SOUL

SEEING WITH THE SOUL

Cover design: Jim Bateman
Cover photograph: Craig Aurness/WestLight
Interior illustrations: Paul Ritscher
First Printing: September 1991 (10)
ISBN 0-8358-0641-3
Library of Congress Catalog Card Number: 91-65726

Printed in the United States of America

"Blessed are the eyes
which see what you see!"
—Luke 10:23

"We do not see with the eye,
but through the eye."
—William Blake

Also by J. Barrie Shepherd

The Moveable Feast:
Selected Poems for the Christian Year and Beyond

A Pilgrim's Way:
Meditations for Lent and Easter

A Child is Born:
Meditations for Advent and Christmas

Praying the Psalms:
Daily Meditations on Cherished Psalms

Prayers from the Mount:
Daily Meditations on the Sermon on the Mount

Encounters:
Poetic Meditations on the Old Testament

A Diary of Prayer:
Daily Meditations on the Parables of Jesus

Diary of Daily Prayer

CONTENTS

PREFACE 9

DAY ONE
 Luke 2:1-12 The First Sign 13
DAY TWO
 Luke 5:1-11 The People Fishers 18
DAY THREE
 Luke 5:27-32 Of Sickness and Health 23
DAY FOUR
 Luke 5:33-35 A Time to Fast 28
DAY FIVE
 Luke 6:39-42 Of Blindness 33
DAY SIX
 Luke 6:46-49 Construction 38
DAY SEVEN
 Luke 7:31-35 Children's Games 43
DAY EIGHT
 Luke 7:36-50 Of Debts and Credits 48
DAY NINE
 Luke 8:16-17 Letting the Light Shine 53
DAY TEN
 Luke 10:1-2 Harvesting 58
DAY ELEVEN
 Luke 10:3-16 Of Lambs and Wolves 63
DAY TWELVE
 Luke 10:17-20 Satan's Fall 68
DAY THIRTEEN
 Luke 10:25-37 About Neighbors 73
DAY FOURTEEN
 Luke 11:9-13 Asking and Receiving 78
DAY FIFTEEN
 Luke 11:14-20 Cross Purposes 83
DAY SIXTEEN
 Luke 12:22-32 Providence 88

DAY SEVENTEEN
      Luke 12:32-34 Treasure 93
DAY EIGHTEEN
      Luke 12:41-48 Stewarding 98
DAY NINETEEN
      Luke 12:54-56 Signs 103
DAY TWENTY
      Luke 13:6-9 Fruit Bearing 108
DAY TWENTY-ONE
      Luke 13:18-19 Mustard Seed 114
DAY TWENTY-TWO
      Luke 13:22-30 The Narrow Door 119
DAY TWENTY-THREE
      Luke 13:31-35 The Mother Hen 124
DAY TWENTY-FOUR
      Luke 14:7-24 The Marriage Feast 130
DAY TWENTY-FIVE
      Luke 14:25-33 Counting the Cost 135
DAY TWENTY-SIX
      Luke 14:34-35 Salt 140
DAY TWENTY-SEVEN
      Luke 15:1-10 Lost and Found 145
DAY TWENTY-EIGHT
      Luke 15:11-32 Father and Sons 150
DAY TWENTY-NINE
      Luke 16:19-31 Dives and Lazarus 155
DAY THIRTY
      Luke 22:14-23 Loaf and Cup 160

Preface

In turning once again to the parables of Jesus—having previously examined them almost ten years ago in my second book, *A Diary of Prayer: Daily Meditations on the Parables of Jesus*—I was, at the outset, somewhat anxious as to whether I would find sufficient new material to fill another volume. Exactly how many parables were there? And would it be permissible to take a second look at parables I had treated in the earlier work? Perhaps I should examine miracles instead; or maybe I should combine miracles and parables as "Signs and Sayings of the Kingdom."

I decided to begin by exploring just one Gospel—Saint Luke—to discover what the potential might be. By the time I had completed this initial probe I had uncovered almost seventy parables in Luke's Gospel alone—from lengthy and carefully constructed stories like the good Samaritan and the prodigal son, all the way to fleeting yet enormously telling images like the hen and her chicks in Luke 13:34 or that brief macabre image of a corpse surrounded by vultures in 17:37—and I was well on my way toward a whole new appreciation of the role of the parables in Jesus' life and ministry.

I quickly realized that there was no way I could hope to do justice to both miracles and parables in one slim volume like this one. There was just too much material. Then it dawned on me that, despite their historic separation into two distinct categories, the miracles and parables of our Lord were not all that clearly separated or delineated and each shared characteristics of the other. Almost all of the miracle stories can be, and have usually been interpreted as acted parables—spectacular ways of disclosing the reality, glory, and purposes of God. Whereas the parables, in their original splendor, beneath the overlay of centuries of familiarity and pious, platitudinous, or moralistic abuse, these parables in their infinite variety, integrity, and startlingly lucid ability to communicate were often nothing less than miracles in verbal form.

The more parables I discovered in Luke, the more I came to realize that these stories and word pictures were not any kind of special teachings set off with capital letters or gold edging from Jesus' other, more everyday sayings. Rather it appears to be the case that Jesus usually tended to talk in parables; to "speak parable," just as someone might speak French, German, or Hebrew. The reason for this, I suspect, was not mere happenstance, or just a personal stylistic preference of the young carpenter from Nazareth. Rather it was that the reality our Lord was seeking to express was most naturally and fluently presented not in theses, commandments, or equations, not in carefully reasoned and logically balanced argumentations; but in pictures drawn from everyday life. Jesus did not *choose* to speak in parables; he could not have said what he said, done what he did, in any other way. Indeed, the truth he came to represent could not be fully and adequately presented in any other way.

What I began to discover is that the essence, not just of Jesus' teachings or miracles, but of his whole ministry and mission was in a fundamental sense *parabolic*. He came to tell us, and show us, that life has another meaning; that just beneath the surface of what we usually call "reality" there is a dimension of depth and wonder awaiting our discovery, a dimension in which the ultimate reality—God—is revealed to all who are willing to see.

Even his greatest and most memorable acts, the Jordan baptism, the Transfiguration, the entry to Jerusalem, the Last Supper, and the Crucifixion itself were all, in one sense, parables: ways, at times agonizingly costly ways, of disclosing the most fundamental truth of all, God's gracious purpose for this whole creation. When Jesus said, "Show me a coin," and went on to use that coin as a parable of our divided loyalties; and when, at that holiest of tables, our Lord uttered the sacred words, "This bread is my body, this cup is my blood," he was "parabling"; he was pouring his very life into the effort to tell us that every single created thing, from the simplest to the most complex, bears within itself, as parable, the ability to communicate the mystery and marvel of God's presence, God's challenge, and God's power.

I finally decided to select parables for this book solely from the Gospel of Saint Luke and to concentrate my thinking not only on familiar tales, but also upon those "lesser parables," the seemingly minor and momentary images, the split-second illustrations which appear to have been typical of all of Jesus' discourse.

It is my sincere hope, then, that as we move together day-by-day through these old and yet ever new images and narratives, we can begin to rediscover for ourselves this parabolic way of seeing reality; that we can learn from Jesus' sayings, not just a bunch of useful information and inspiring thoughts, but an entirely new perspective on this world in which we live and this Lord we seek to serve.

Two practical notes before launching out:

Part of the usefulness of a prayer diary such as this is its ability to stimulate the reader to formulate his or her own prayers and meditations. I have suggested a scripture passage for each day to be read before launching into the actual meditation. And then, as in my other books, I have endeavored to leave some free space on the page so that you, the reader/pray-er, can set down reflections and be encouraged to bring forth your own images, to exercise the gift of parabolic vision for yourself.

Much of this book was written during an extended study leave spent in a log cabin on a rocky island off the Maine coast. Scenes, incidents, and characters from the life of that island are drawn upon in many of the meditations. The name and precise location of the island will remain, of course, a closely guarded secret.

I wish to express my thanks to all who had a part in the inspiration and preparation of these meditations: the friends who permeate these pages, the family—wife, Mhairi, and daughters, Alison, Fiona, Nicola, and Catriona who participated in many of the incidents. They too have become for me, at times, parables—revelations of the presence of the Divine at the heart of everyday life. I would dedicate this book, however, to the coastal people of Scotland and Maine—fishers and farmers, carpenters and shepherds—and to the living creatures, the flora and fauna of those magical regions. I do this in fond remembrance and deep gratitude for the lessons they have taught, for the life and the world they have illumined from within.

DAY ONE
The First Sign
Luke 2:1-12

DAY ONE/Morning

And this will be a sign for you . . .
—Luke 2:1-12

Did the whole thing then
begin with a parable?
Not to suggest, of course,
that this didn't really happen;
that these birth narratives are just
a lovely legend thought up by the early church;
not even to enter into
that whole ancient, scholarly,
and finally rather pointless debate;
but might it not be
that just as with his teachings,
so in this poignant moment of his birth—
the scandal for poor Mary, Joseph too,
the untimely journey and unlikely setting,
no room at the inn and the immediate shadow
of a sword across his infant cradle—
might it not be that here,
right at the outset
God was giving us a sign,
a preview, as it were,
of all that was to follow;
and that in his triumphant escape
from beneath the shadow of death,
in this initial glad outwitting
of the dread powers of evil
we gain a glimpse, a fleeting foretaste
of that final, splendid, ultimate
and almost incredible outcome?

"And this will be a sign . . ."
the angel said.
Not just the humble birth,
cowshed and manger, but this whole
"Christ the Lord . . . born to you this day,"
what the scholars call "The Christ Event"
from start to finish—
the stable to the stone that rolled away—

this entire lifetime,
this history, this breaking
into history of dizzying eternity;
all this will be a sign to you and me.

And so it was;
angels seldom get it wrong.
The things he said and did as he grew up,
the life he lived, the death he died,
not only was, but is today a sign,
if we will heed it—
a sign that tells us
there is more to life
than may appear to be evident
at first glance;
a sign that points
beyond itself to something,
someone vaster,
more simple yet complex,
more loving, more forgiving,
more life-creating and life-giving
than we could ever hope for, wish for,
dream of in our maddest fantasies.

As I begin this new day, Lord,
open my eyes and ears,
all my senses, however many,
to the signs that will surround me,
to the glory that lies just below the surface,
to your sacred, hidden presence
within everything that is.
Amen.

DAY ONE/Evening

And this will be a sign for you . . .
—Luke 2:1-12

Last summer,
while visiting old friends
in the medieval city of Saint Flour
in south central France,
we spent an afternoon looking at houses.
One in particular was located
almost opposite the home of our hosts,
Jean and Guy,
on a winding, cobbled street
entirely lined with buildings
from the fourteenth century.

We had noticed the sign,
Maison à Vendre (house for sale)
as we climbed the steep and narrow way
to buy our morning croissants,
the *baguettes* for later on,
fragrant-fresh from the brick ovens
at the old *boulangerie;*
and so we got the key
from the office of the *avocat*
and went to have a look.
But the door from the street wouldn't budge.
We tried this way and that,
pulling and pushing,
each one taking a turn and getting nowhere.
Finally, in mock desperation,
I cried, "Open Sesame!"
threw myself against the door
and flipped the key hard,
but it was no good.
The thing stayed shut.
Then Guy stepped forward,
took the key and said,
"It's a French door after all,
Sésame ouvre-toi!"
and the stubborn door swung wide and free.

16

We had quite a laugh about that French door;
but later, looking back,
I found another meaning in that moment.
What we had needed, or so it seemed,
was the right word,
in the right language.
And is that not also what we need today?
Like those Bethlehem shepherds we seek for signs.
We check forecasts for the weather,
the economy, peruse our daily horoscope,
maintain a careful watch over health,
appearance, ranking in the many pecking orders.
Despite the world-weary facade we learn to wear,
we scan our world for signs of hope, progress,
meaning—yearning for something to believe in,
dedicate our lives to,
beyond the dreary grind of sheer survival.

Yet this old story would suggest
the sign has been already given,
the right Word in the right language
has been already spoken;
and if we would find
the key that can unlock
this mysterious house of consciousness,
permit us to roam free, explore,
and come to know its many rooms,
then we should look no further than a manger
and a fishing boat, a wildflower-scattered hillside
and a blood-bespattered cross.

While I sleep this night, O Lord,
unlock the door
that bars me from your presence.
May I rise to walk a world which lies
wide open to the splendors and the mystery
of your grace.
Amen.

DAY TWO
The People Fishers
Luke 5:1-11

Do not be afraid; henceforth you will be catching men.
—Luke 5:1-11

Again, this is not
one of the "classic" parables.
Some might question
whether it is a parable at all.
But this powerful image
drawn from the daily working world
of Jesus' audience,
this metaphor of fishing pervades
not just the Gospel narratives,
but the creative imagination
of the whole church down the ages.
One of the favorite gospel songs of my youth:
        I will make you fishers of men . . .
continues this tradition,
conjuring to the mind's eye
scenes of strong fisherfolk,
hauling on the nets,
rejoicing in God's bounty from the sea.

Simon and his friends
had fished all night with empty nets.
Rising with the July sun,
I launch out from the shore
below our Maine island cottage
trying to catch breakfast.
There are days,
not too many, thank the Lord,
when I return empty-handed,
or rather empty-pailed,
when I share the disappointment Simon felt.
But then, I am not fishing for my living.

Over more than twenty summers
I have been fortunate to come to know
some of our island's fishing families,
people whose livelihoods revolve
around the sea and all its creatures.

DAY TWO/Morning

I have learned to respect their independence,
their frugal, hard-working ways,
their skill and hard-won knowledge
of tides, currents, wind, and weather,
their persistent cheerfulness,
often in face of hardship and true danger,
their fierce loyalty to one another,
and their ancient trade.
And I wonder,
in terms of Jesus' imagery
and of his life-long familiarity
with this hardy way of life,
I wonder how the church might learn from
"those who go down to the sea in ships."

To be like fisherfolk we must
admit again the fact of our dependence.
Cocooned in cities, suburbs,
we come to believe that we are in control,
that our efforts and abilities
will determine our future.
Those who reap the ocean's harvest
know just enough to realize that,
for all their ancient skills,
they are dependent upon powers
far beyond themselves.
They live closer to the facts
of life and death, survival and disaster.

Grant me, O God, the honesty,
humility, and courage to live my days
in full awareness of my frailty and folly,
your majesty and might.
And mold me in the model
of those fisherfolk of old;
through Christ who holds me in his net
so that I need not be afraid.
Amen.

Do not be afraid; henceforth you will be catching men.
—Luke 5:1-11

Jesus' image in this mini-parable,
this whole metaphor of "catching men,"
raises for the church the topic of evangelism.
To be "fishers of men" has simply meant,
for many Christians,
persuading other people to accept
without question their own understanding
of everything Jesus said and did.

It is difficult,
perhaps even impossible,
to be sure what Jesus originally meant
when he spoke this parable;
but I do wonder whether
he could really have had in mind
the modern-day, high-powered
evangelistic crusade,
or the vast financial empires
of mass media televangelism.

To be those who fish for people
(and it does not do to take
the metaphor too literally, otherwise
we end up with blood on our hands!),
to be Jesus' kind of fisherfolk,
we need to look at the changes he actually made
in the lives of those to whom he made this promise.
Simon Peter would seem the prime example:
and far from setting himself up
as a professional preacher and soul-saver,
Peter appears to have spent his days
just trying to stick close to Jesus,
despite a whole host of personal
and various other problems
which continually got in the way.
He let his master down
on more than one occasion,

seemed to have a genuine talent
for saying the wrong thing at the wrong time
and for impetuous, ill-advised action,
and yet he is remembered to this day
as one of the great founders
of the early church.

Andrew too,
as far as we can learn from the Gospels,
was never one to make a fuss,
never one who could stand up in public,
make a stirring speech, or draw attention to himself.
Andrew was something of a bridge-builder,
or a go-between—a "contact person"
we might call him nowadays—
always seeing to it that others
got the chance to meet and listen to
this One who lived and taught the way of life,
this One whose voice had called him
from his nets onto the open road.

For all their failings and mistakes
these very first disciples were devoted to Jesus,
desired to follow him in all they did,
and finally gave up their lives
following in his footsteps.
And they were "fishers of men."

Show me how to win others to your side,
Lord Christ, not with empty promises
or fearful "terror-tactics"
threatening damnation and hellfire,
but through a daily life that shows
some of that abundance, grace, and joy,
that passionate concern for others,
that communion with the realm of the divine
that drew men and women to you,
still draws me now, this very night.
Amen.

DAY THREE
Of Sickness and Health
Luke 5:27-32

Those who are well have no need of a physician, but those who are sick.

—Luke 5:27-32

In Sunday school we always learned
to despise the Pharisees.
It has only been recently,
at a much later date,
that I have caught the irony
in our despising those who despised others!

In reading the latest studies
of New Testament life and times;
and in learning to listen to
my scholar friend, our local rabbi,
I have had to face the fact that the Pharisees
were really rather admirable people.
They were the enlightened Jews,
those who took their religion so seriously
they turned all their intelligence,
education and determination to the task
of making it a living reality.
They were not wicked or evil people,
nor were they necessarily all that proud,
self-righteous, or intolerant.
From all we can learn they were
the would-be-good people of Jesus' time,
those who sought to live an upright life,
to maintain standards, to worship God
in a decent, orderly manner.

One can understand,
surely, how they might object
when someone came among them,
claiming to stand for, even to fulfill
everything they cherished and strove after,
yet spending time with those whose habits,
occupations, ways of life seemed to deny
and work against those values.
It's a bit like those of us

who are so concerned about fitness,
health and preventive medicine nowadays.
We become so committed, so involved,
so personally engaged in this important cause,
we have no time for those who will not join us,
those who persist in ruining their lungs—
ours too—by smoking cigarettes.

Not only this, but we begin,
if we're not careful, to believe
that by strenuous discipline and effort
we can beat the odds, make ourselves immortal.
So supremely fit, how could we ever need a doctor?
Until one day, soon or late, the reaper's blade
is turned in our surprised direction.
"You won't live any longer,
but you'll enjoy it so much more."
That's how one physician spoke to me of exercise.
But we forget and thus forfeit the very lives
we seek to save in struggling to stay fit.

Jesus' words are not for those
who believe they are in pretty good shape.
They are too fit, too sure of their well-being
to ever heed his offer of God's help.
You have to need good news to hear it,
you have to see that you require help
in order to receive it.
We need to recognize our death
before we can see through to life beyond.

Show me what really matters, Lord,
help me to distinguish means from ends,
life itself from mere preparation or protection.
Teach me to be good,
without trusting in goodness,
to stay fit while still entrusting
my eternal health into your gracious care.
Amen.

Those who are well have no need of a physician, but those who are sick.

—Luke 5:27-32

These sick ones
to whom Jesus actually came,
were they, then, better off?
Is it more advantageous,
even more commendable in gospel terms,
to be in desperate moral health—
a notorious ethical failure,
a crook, cheat, or liar,
one who sells body, mind, or soul—
because then one, at least,
has something to repent of?

Or might Jesus really have meant
to say what he appeared to say
—setting irony aside for the moment—
that those who were "well" did not need him,
were already in a healthy relationship with God,
and that his actual redemptive mission
was restricted solely to those
who could make it in no other way?

Yet many of his other parables and teachings,
his fierce, scathing comments
to those who considered they had no need of him,
suggest this was not the case.
Far from seeking to assign
any kind of gospel classification—
either superior or inferior—
to those whose moral failure was
most blatant or flagrantly evident,
most available for public scandal
and open denunciation,
Jesus seems to have been saying,
proclaiming loud and clear to one and all,
that the sickness he has come to cure
is a universal and omnipresent disease,

yet one not recognized as such.
It is an ailment afflicting equally
those who believe they are morally upright,
and those who are sure they are not.
In fact, this illness goes beyond morality
to the central question of all being,
that of relationship to God.

Jesus taught,
and showed in his life,
that our standing with God
is not based on our relative goodness
or comparative wickedness,
but rather on God's sovereign grace
and our acceptance of divine mercy.

Thus it was that those who knew
they did not have a moral leg to stand on
were already one step ahead, as it were,
of all who trusted in their own good name.
Those who were most obviously sick
were by that very fact rendered
more ready to admit their need,
submit their lives
to the stringent remedy
prescribed by our Lord.

Preserve me, great Physician,
from trusting in my own prescriptions,
from attempting to cure myself.
Heal me with your touch,
mend me with your wonder-working hands,
then guide me forth to live
a healed and whole and holy life
that springs fresh from your mercy.
Amen.

DAY FOUR
A Time to Fast
Luke 5:33-35

Can you make wedding guests fast while the bridegroom is
with them? The days will come, when the bridegroom is taken
away from them, and then they will fast in those days.
—Luke 5:33-35

So many of Jesus' parables
are set around a wedding feast
or a festive royal banquet.
This brief glimpse of such a scene
is focused on the idea of fasting
as an appropriate discipline for the soul.

In response to those who murmur
at the less-than-solemn ways of his followers,
Jesus points out that discipleship
has its varied and contrasting seasons.
As Koheleth, the writer of Ecclesiastes,
might have said many centuries before:
> *There is a time to fast*
> *and a time to feast*
and it is important to know
just which is proper and fitting
for the moment.

For some time now—
several centuries with Protestants—
fasting has been clearly out of favor
as a form of spiritual exercise.
The people of the Reformation
saw fasting as a relic
left over from their Roman Catholic past,
a somewhat meaningless method
of trying to earn merit,
to bank up favor with God,
rather than relying on the free
and generous grace of Christ alone.

Again in our era,
with the bold new insights
of the psychologists into the human psyche,

all such traditional "mortifications of the flesh"
have come to be viewed as serious indications
of instability, unhealthy masochism,
or self-punishment;
as clear signs of mental illness.

In recent years, however,
partly as a result of dietary consciousness
—excess concern about excess weight—
but also as a dramatic form
of political and ethical protest and dissent,
fasting has been gaining favor once again;
although it is usually undertaken without
any explicit spiritual dimension.

Even within the church today,
in prayer groups and study circles,
there seems to be a renewed interest
in this time-honored method for
taking control of one's body
—harnessing and subduing
one's physical needs and desires—
and reaching out to God.

Help me to avoid, Lord God,
the arrogant and life-denying folly
of selecting and inflicting
my own punishment,
thus trying to earn forgiveness.
But teach me to appreciate
the lessons to be learned
from self-purification:
cutting down distractions,
limiting my satisfactions
to the barest of essentials,
and thus coming to appreciate
how little I really need;
how much you freely give.
Amen.

*Can you make wedding guests fast while the bridegroom is
with them? The days will come, when the bridegroom is taken
away from them, and then they will fast in those days.*
—Luke 5:33-35

Even when they are not fasting
too many Christians have a tendency
to look and act as though they were.
Somehow, over the centuries,
the followers of Jesus have contrived
to squeeze most of the original rejoicing
out of the gospel message
and replace it with pale lemon juice.

The Puritans must bear some responsibility for this,
with their austere, frowning disapproval
of all sorts of frivolous pursuits;
but long before the Puritans
the Christian faith was seen by its opponents
as a killjoy, a wet blanket heavy draped
over every human possibility for fun.
"Far too many Christians,"
as a friend of mine once put it,
"wear a face like a week of wet Mondays."
The irony of it is, of course,
that Jesus and his friends were accused
of the very opposite kind of attitude:
of being happy-go-lucky, high-living types
who lived as if life was a party
that had only just begun.

What is the proper Christian posture?
Should we fast or feast,
frown severely, grin inanely,
regard the world with caution
as a place of trial and testing,
or embrace God's glorious creation
with open arms and grateful hearts?
Jesus suggests there are times
for each alternative.

DAY FOUR/Evening

And in our day,
after long decades of doom and gloom,
solemnity that verged upon morbidity,
sanctuaries with all the light
and warmth of a typical funeral parlor,
the church is beginning to rediscover joy,
to reclaim its heritage of celebration,
affirmation, and glad praise.

This joy, however,
cannot be forced or counterfeit.
Fake happiness—along with pretend love—
is just about the falsest thing there is,
and one of the easiest to detect.
So many of the Christians I see on television
wear smiles that look as pasted-on
as those in any toothpaste commercial!
The joy lived daily by our Lord,
that steadfast, sure rejoicing
that undergirded everything he said and did,
tended to be a quality of life which rose,
not from the denial of the ugly side,
from fleeing the reality of suffering,
but rather out of facing life
in all its contradictions,
sharing the hurt of others,
tackling with ruthless honesty
the tough, unanswerable questions
that plague both mind and conscience,
and giving thanks because, despite it all,
the Lord is good, our days are in God's hands.

Set your joy firm in me tonight,
that joy in which you formed the earth
and sent your Son to call us home.
Let the radiance of his cross
illumine all these hours of rest,
and lead me forth to service in the morning.
Amen.

DAY FIVE
Of Blindness
Luke 6:39-42

DAY FIVE/Morning

Can a blind man lead a blind man? Will they not both fall into a pit?

—Luke 6:39-42

Here we find one of our typical brief "story-sayings"
actually identified by Luke as a parable.
In fact, this identification introduces
a series of such short, vivid sayings:
the blind leading the blind,
the disciple and the teacher,
the speck and the log,
the good tree and the bad.

This morning,
just after sunrise,
I went fishing in the fog.
I say "just after sunrise"
because we could actually glimpse the sun
at times, a pale, moon-like disc,
its partly veiled face glistening
above the banks of moisture.

There is nothing quite like a Maine coast fog.
I knew British "pea-soupers" as a child
during the war, but they were darker,
smokier, much harder on the throat.
Maine fog is light and luminous,
yet dense, so that you think
you can see further than you can.
Objects—lobster buoys, boats,
birds and rocky ledges—
will suddenly appear,
much closer to you than they ought to be.
And when all objects disappear—
when there is nothing to be seen
but gray-green water all around,
for all your intent, semi-anxious gaze,
and this continues five, ten,
fifteen minutes at a stretch
of eerie stillness, absence,

damp and chilly emptiness—
then you begin to ask yourself
whether your compass can be right,
or if, perhaps, they moved the island
overnight while you were sleeping.

Once, years ago,
we almost ran a boat onto the rocks
because the captain—
full professor of psychology, no less—
would not believe his compass,
insisted upon relying on his own,
lifelong "unerring" sense of direction
till it was just about too late.
I guess that really was the blind
leading the blind!

There are worse things
than a Maine coastal fog.
There is a mist envelopes mind and spirit,
shutting off direction, closing down communication,
leaving one with nothing, no one,
to reach out to or seek guidance from.
There is a lostness will not clear
like early morning vapor,
an emptiness the rising sun
can never burn away,
a blindness will not see the signs,
the hand stretched out, door set open.
There is a fear of being left alone,
adrift, eternally alone.

Stay close beside me this new day,
my Saviour, Guide, and Pilot.
Chart my course in waters broad and deep,
and beneath clear, blue skies.
Then moor me—safe at last—
within the harbor.
Amen.

Can a blind man lead a blind man? Will they not both fall into a pit?

—Luke 6:39-42

Here on the island in Maine
our closest friends, the Todds,
have a son who is blind.
Jimmy Todd has been blind for years,
the result of German Measles
during his mother's pregnancy.
Yet in this close-drawn community,
and within the limits of his condition,
Jimmy copes superbly.

He knows the island roads
and paths by heart,
recognizes voices instantly,
knits heads for lobster traps
to earn pocket money,
and is a mine of ready
and accurate information on tides,
telephone numbers, island lore,
and all the local gossip.
You can even ask him for directions
to various locations on the island
and he will keep you on the right track.
But I would not invite him
to come along and be my guide.

The trouble is, as Jesus saw it,
that some of those
most eager to guide others
will not admit they are themselves
completely without sight.
People counsel other people,
while they themselves live lives
of quiet, secret desolation and despair.
The so-called successes of our culture,
role models for the rest of us—
athletes, entertainers, talk-show hosts,

and billion-dollar speculators—
offer their glistening pearls of wisdom,
the glossy distilled platitudes of hours
and years of television trivia,
to their mass media followers,
and are hailed as new messiahs,
revealers of as yet undiscovered truth.

"Will they not both fall into a pit?"
the pit where people grope around in darkness,
push and crush and trample one another;
the pit where no one can climb out
because of others clambering up their backs
trying to do the same;
the pit where all is lost until someone with vision,
one who sees the light and also shares it,
will reach down and seize a hand
and start to pull.

There are such persons in our world,
but they are not often seen on television
or in the best-seller charts.
People nowadays seem to crave comfort
and diversion rather than enlightenment;
and in the consumer society
what people crave is usually what people get.
Yet for those who walk with open eyes
and hopeful, expectant hearts,
the light still shines,
the truth still beckons,
the way still opens up before them.

My eyes are dim, Lord,
I need your guidance for my daily walk.
Set my feet upon a plain path,
and make clear your holy way before me.
In Christ, the living Way.
Amen.

DAY SIX
Construction
Luke 6:46-49

He is like a man building a house . . .
                    —Luke 6:46-49

A couple of days ago,
while scraping the front porch
before applying a fresh coat of paint
I noticed the scraper sinking
into the wood just a bit too easily,
just a bit further than it should.

Investigation led to the discovery
that the foundations of that corner,
the once-strong timbers which had held
the building firm for over twenty years,
were crumbling with dry rot.
I could lift away whole sections
with my fingertips.

An island carpenter stopped by
and pointed out how this had happened.
Wild rugosa rose bushes I had planted close
along the ocean-facing section of the building
had kept the wind from battering the place
but had also held the moisture in,
stopped the boards from fully drying out
after the fierce winter storms.
A finish board along the sill
had been left half-an-inch too short,
and so the rain had penetrated in below
rather than dropping off onto the ground.
And I remembered, during earlier summers,
as I had scraped and painted those same boards,
noticing a softness—a "punkiness"—
there in the wood and deciding to ignore it,
leave it for another day.

Carelessness, ignorance, neglect,
I had not realized what I was getting into.
Those rose bushes, after all,
were planted with the best intentions,

beauty and protection, both combined.
Yet their blossoms came at a price
I now would have to pay.

Dry rot is a condition
that afflicts the firm foundations
of human souls as well as summer cottages.
It can begin with something planned
as an improvement, some delightful new addition
to add color, break up harshness, and even,
incidentally, bring a layer of protection
from the occasional winter storm.
It may continue through neglect,
an unwillingness to recognize
the early signs and symptoms of decay,
putting off replacements and repairs until
another more convenient season.
It can end up in disaster
with relationships, reputation,
self-respect, health, and even
life itself—eternity, no less,
all hanging in the balances.

You know, O Divine Carpenter,
the condition of my soul.
Your expert eye detects those places—
far too many, I am certain—
that may be soft and crumbling
and requiring prompt attention.
Join your craftsman's hands to mine
to help me build a structure
that can stand the tests
of tempest and of time,
until you welcome me
into that house not made with hands,
the heavenly home in which,
I pray, you have prepared
a place for me.
Amen.

He is like a man building a house . . .
                         —Luke 6:46-49
I picked up the lumber yesterday
to replace the rotting timbers of our porch;
borrowed an old rusty pickup truck
from Andrew the lobsterman
while he was on the water hauling traps,
drove down to the wharf through driving rain—
careful on that slippery dock far out into the cove—
and loaded on the pressure-treated pieces
delivered earlier that morning by the boat
that serves the islands of our bay.

There is something about new lumber—
even when it's wet with rain
and the resin smell is partly washed away—
something about new lumber
that makes my soul begin to sing.
Maybe it's the potential of it,
the lively invitation to shape raw,
new timber into walls and windows,
porches, doors, and roofs.
Or could it be a primitive urge
to fashion shelter
from the natural provisions
of God's earth?
I feel the weight, the heft,
the yield, the flexible yet solid strength
of two-by-eights, spruce decking and pine boards,
and fingers itch for saw and level,
ruler, hammer, and nails.

What is there in my life
that brings this strength,
this suppleness, this tough,
yet yielding, firm enduring quality,
and even something of this sheer delight?
What materials has my builder-God provided
with which to undergird the sagging soul?

There are the hopes,
good hopes that never fail completely,
hopes for peace and trust and love,
a life that makes a difference,
a joy that conquers fear.

There are the loves
of family and friends,
those with whom we struggle
and make up across the course of years,
of decades; the gifts and strengths
that love has brought,
will still bring in the future;
humility, the acceptance of vulnerability—
even failure—honest tenderness both given
and received, genuine self-knowledge,
and the occasional glimpse of victory,
of realistic, true self-worth,
and momentary ecstasy.

There is the faith,
the prayers we learned
on bended knee beside the childhood bed;
heroic figures touched by God that we looked up to;
stories we stored up around the family fireside:
a long, maturing lifeline to this One
whom we call Jesus, whose living
and whose dying we can never quite forget;
whose words and attitudes to life
shape all we do, and even
all we do not do.

Take these foundations, Lord,
and in these hours of sleep
renew my footing firm upon them.
Then let me rise restored in faith
and hope and love, in Christ, through Christ.
Amen.

DAY SEVEN
Children's Games
Luke 7:31-35

They are like children sitting in the market place and calling to one another . . .

—Luke 7:31-35

These children in Jesus' parable
are playing at a game,
an old, familiar,
ever-popular, time-tested,
yet constantly updated
and perfected little game.
It is the game called "Criticism"
and consists of listing one's complaints,
one's critical and negative evaluations,
as a safe and certain-sure way
to avoid facing the issue.

The critics of the faith
play this game all the time, asking:
Why are Christians so contentious?
Why are priests and preachers never perfect?
What about the institutional church
with its slow and cumbersome procedures;
its seemingly enormous hoarded assets;
its hierarchies of rank and show;
pomp, privilege, and power;
its continual division
into ever smaller,
ever more irrelevant
sects and clans
and parties?
And then, of course,
there are those hypocrites
who inhabit church pews every Sunday—
what has the faith to say about all those?

Turning to the past they ask,
Who was it carried out the Inquisition,
the Crusades, and the pogroms;
burned the heretics and witches;
fought those dreadful, never-ending holy wars?

Who was it that resisted over centuries
the new and shattering insights
of the scientists and scholars?
So they fling their angry questions
at the church, the faith, the Lord,
and yet, just like anxious Pilate,
with his question, "What is truth?"
they never seem to wait for,
or even want to hear an answer.

Yet even as believers,
those who do their best to follow Christ,
we too play at this game.
We raise and then prolong our
theological and ethical debates,
concentrating on the most obscure points
in order to avoid having to do something,
change our lives perhaps, in response
to evident truths that stare us in the face.
So we pick and poke and argue,
oh so very nicely, from the sidelines,
finding ways we can escape
the searching question Jesus poses
simply by being, and being here beside us.

Lord, when all our games are over,
you remain the living truth,
in a cradle, on a cross,
beside the road, across the table
or the desk, in the marketplace
where people gather to exchange their gifts
and needs, even in this ordinary place
where I kneel to begin another day.
As I go out preserve me, Lord,
from foolish and evasive games.
Let me answer your question
with myself.
Amen.

They are like children sitting in the market place and calling to one another . . .

—Luke 7:31-35

When Jesus told his followers
they must become again
like little children,
I do not think this kind of behavior
is exactly what he had in mind.
There is, after all,
a whole lifestyle of difference
between being childlike
and being childish.

Rather than the petulance,
the whining and malcontent complaints
of the young people in this parable,
surely the intent of Jesus
was to call people to recapture
the directness and simplicity,
the lack of pompous self-importance,
the spontaneity and sheer ability to respond,
in a truly profound sense,
the joyful poverty of children.
Only in such a frame of mind and heart
can we see and grasp the life he offers
with genuine enthusiasm
and with no reservations whatsoever.

On the other hand,
our days become so cluttered
with genuinely childish nonsense:
those vital yet voracious details—
life-consuming, if we are not careful—
of providing daily bread and meat and shelter
(plus, of course, a few optional extras!),
the constant jockeying for position,
promotion, power, and prestige
that keeps us ever with a watchful eye
on the performance of the rest of the field;

the pursuit of entertainments
to divert our weary hearts and minds,
our fearfully empty souls,
from all these other devilish concerns;
our endless searching for
and grasping after a security
we can never hope to find
this side, our side,
of that reality we seldom name,
yet all must meet,
called death.

Sometimes it seems
the more years I accumulate,
the closer I creep back to
the narrow selfishness
of crib and nursery,
the complete
and almost frightening
absorption with sheer survival
that controls the babe in arms.

Receive back
this dying day now, Lord.
Let the velvet, cleansing
curtain of your night
sweep away all I have done
in the pursuit of pointlessness
and futile, selfish gain.
Grant me,
in this closing hour,
a clear and childlike vision
of your purity and grace,
to prepare me for my resting
and for the road ahead.
Amen.

DAY EIGHT
Of Debts and Credits
Luke 7:36-50

A certain creditor had two debtors . . .
                                    —Luke 7:36-50
What a brief and telling parable this is:
in swift and economical strokes
Jesus paints an entire living drama
of despair, doom, and deliverance,
and all to ask this Simon,
this generous,
yet unforgiving Pharisee,
a question about love.

If I were suddenly required
to pay my debts to God,
called upon, without prior notice,
to settle the accounts
with my Creator and Redeemer,
what would I have to answer for?
How could I begin to tally up
the extent of my indebtedness?

What value should I place,
for example, on the first sweet breath
of fragrance in the springtime;
or those towering, golden hallways,
the dreaming treetop palaces of fall?
What would I pay back for music,
for melody, rhythm, harmony,
supplying the deep wellsprings
of the human spirit;
or for the vital nourishment
of drama, art, and poetry?
Might there somehow be
a valid price to recompense
for sunset-shouldered mountains
and the moving, mysterious,
and ever-beckoning sea?

Could I find a way to pay for
all the vast accumulated heritage

DAY EIGHT/Morning

of learning and tradition,
splendid treasures of the past,
discoveries still waiting to be made?
And what about the comforts,
those support-systems that surround me,
warm and cool and cosset me,
providing for so many daily needs
and necessaries without my even noticing;
or, again, this mostly-willing body
which, for all it's passing aches and pains,
has served me long and well across
the span of more than fifty years?

What, precisely, do I owe for love
which tendered me through infancy and childhood,
put up with me through adolescence,
endured the troubled, anxious middle years,
supports and struggles with me still
in such a rich variety of ways through family,
friends, community, and church?

And how much should I reimburse for faith?
a church and company to serve in and be served by,
a holy sanctuary space for mystery and awe,
a table at which everyone is welcomed and is fed,
a book in which to trace the light of truth,
the paths of life and death,
a Lord who will not let me fall forever?

You know, Lord, that I cannot pay,
cannot even begin to assess my debt to you
and to your grace in Christ my Saviour.
Yet, in that grace, you tell me to forget
all my indebtedness, tear up the bill,
accept your gifts, and live in them
with joy and gratitude.
Even so, in this true freedom,
may I spend myself this day.
Amen.

A certain creditor had two debtors . . .
—Luke 7:36-50

In this tiny,
tightly-woven vignette
of debts, debtors, and deliverance,
Jesus is trying to teach Simon the Pharisee,
his host, about the nature of forgiveness
and the immediate, intimate link
between forgiveness and love.

As I look back
across the hours of this day,
as I allow the message of this parable
to search out the nooks and crannies,
the secret, hidden corners
of my habits and impulses,
my thoughts, affections, attitudes,
I realize that this quality of forgiveness
has been, for me as it was for Simon,
a gift that is seldom shared.

So much of daily living
can quickly come to be built on grudges,
hurts, long festering resentments.
Indeed, it often seems to me as if,
the closer I draw to someone else,
the more difficult it becomes
to exercise forgiveness.
Total strangers
who defraud, rob, or deceive me,
mere passing acquaintances
who contrive to offend in some way or other,
present me with no major problem.
But with colleagues at work,
close neighbors,
those with whom I pass my leisure time,
fellow members of societies and clubs,
even churches—especially churches—
forgiveness among these has tended

DAY EIGHT/Evening

to become a rare, endangered species.
And with the members of my family,
those nearest, dearest,
and often all too clearest,
there are so many potential provocations,
so many occasions for friction,
that forgiveness becomes simply
a device for getting by,
a way of avoiding ugly explosions,
a survival technique, to be sure,
but one with little time for reconciliation.

There are the faceless grudges, too,
which gash and grind against the spirit;
grudges against the politicians and the poor,
those above us, those below
on the social and economic scale,
all the folk we punish in our prisons
or our welfare/workfare schemes.
Can we forgive the elderly
for being feeble, old, and wrinkled,
reminding us of what we will become,
if we are fortunate?
Can we forgive the young for being right
at times, for reminding us that
we were once like them,
too long ago now?
Can I forgive myself
for not living out my dreams,
for years of quiet compromise with failure?

Deliver me this night, Lord God,
from the prison bars I set around my days,
the jailhouse of resentments and old fears.
Let me taste the sweet new freedom of forgiveness,
forgiveness given and received, in Christ,
to open up the doors to love.
Amen.

DAY NINE
Letting the Light Shine
Luke 8:16-17

DAY NINE/Morning

No one after lighting a lamp covers it with a vessel, or puts it under a bed, but puts it on a stand, that those who enter may see the light.

—Luke 8:16-17

Late summer evenings here in Maine
I will dig out our old lamp collection,
clean up the bright glass lantern chimneys,
trim the wicks, top up the tanks
with scented oil and, sitting in the fireglow,
recapture for an hour or two the softer, gentler,
richly textured lights of earlier times.
There is a magical quality about lamplight
that has been lost in our more convenient days
of instant illumination at the flick of a switch.

Matthew too records this parable about lamps
but places it within another setting
and with a somewhat different application.
Both evangelists, however, make the same basic point,
that light exists to be seen, not hidden away.

Yet there has always been
a tendency among Jesus' followers
to conceal whatever light they have received,
at times out of a wish to keep its wisdom
and enlightenment to themselves;
at times more out of cowardice and fear
of what people might think of them,
do to them, when they realize they are Christians.
It was Peter, at the very start,
in the darkness of the high priest's courtyard,
who found it safer and far more convenient
to linger in the shadows and deny
that he had ever seen any light.

Since that time, the church that Peter founded
has devised its various ways to cover up
the light entrusted to its care.
We have walled it into buildings,

structures, hierarchies, traditions,
creeds, law codes, and libraries of books.
In seeking to define the light,
refine our understanding of its meaning,
applications, implications, and conclusions,
the result has all too often been
to confine the light and keep it to ourselves.
We tend the home fires first, and seldom,
if ever, get around to shedding light
where it is needed most—
not just in the corners where we are
but also where the shadows fall the deepest.
And then we ask ourselves why the lamp
needs so much tending.

What more stupid place to put a lamp
than underneath a tight-sealed vessel?
What more useless way to treat the gospel
of God's bright and liberating light—
that frees us from the fear of darkness,
reveals the power of God's forgiveness,
shows us precisely where we stand
and the universal company we stand in—
than to shut it off, away from those
who stumble in the night.
For as we keep the light from others
we create a deep new darkness for ourselves.
No lamp lives long unless it breathes
the open, full, fresh air of freedom.
No light shines in the darkness
unless it shines for all.

Like the gleam of this new dawn, Lord God,
help me to pierce the darkness
with the light you have entrusted to my keeping.
Teach me to bring your light to all I greet
and every task I undertake this day.
Amen.

DAY NINE/Evening

No one after lighting a lamp covers it with a vessel, or puts it under a bed, but puts it on a stand, that those who enter may see the light.

—Luke 8:16-17

After a few days
of island living here in Maine,
all one's clocks begin to change.
The sense of healing isolation,
that subtly insulating gap
of separation from the mainland,
first detaches
then attunes the spirit, body too,
to older, much more basic calendars and rhythms.
High tide and low tide mark
their ages-old divisions in the day.
One wakens to the sunrise chorus of the birds.
One tumbles, weary, into bed
not too long after sunset.

Each night before I sleep
I take a brief turn out of doors,
step to the edge that overlooks the bay,
and search out the familiar lights
that gleam across the water.
Two miles and more away,
just off the mouth of Royal River,
I note the intermittent flashing green
of the channel entrance marker buoy.
It reassures me,
knowing it's still there;
a sign of constancy hard on the edge
of treacherous shifting sands.

The light that Jesus speaks of here
must surely be like that,
sending forth its strong and secure signal
to announce, "All's well, voyager!
The way is clear. Just follow where I guide
and you will end up safe at anchor."

My fishing partner nowadays,
a sceptical, tough-minded,
highly argumentative research physicist,
is wont to bellow forth,
when the sea is smooth,
the sun is bright and the boat
loaded down with fresh caught giant blues:
> *Let the lower lights be burning!*
> *Send a gleam across the wave!*
as if recapturing raptures
of sunny childhood days, long gone,
when songs like those,
and lights like those shone bright and clear,
their gleaming still undimmed.

We need lamps to guide us now,
harbor lights and beacons
to warn us and direct;
yet those who seem to have the light
are loath to share it, not wishing to impose,
hesitant to press their views on others.
There are also those who are so sure
they have the light, and they alone,
yet all their light is focused on themselves
and darkness clings about their heels.

Teach me, Light of the World,
with whatever light I have received,
to shed illumination, never on myself,
but on your world, your Word,
your will for me and all your children.
Help me to light a path
away from self
and toward Christ,
the everlasting Light.
Amen.

DAY TEN
Harvesting
Luke 10:1-2

The harvest is plentiful, but the laborers are few . . .
—Luke 10:1-2

Traveling across western Europe
as a family four summers ago,
we watched people making hay
the old-fashioned way,
with scythes and sickles, pitchforks too,
even horse-drawn wagons in some places
to haul the harvest from the fields.

Their farming methods were,
we noted, much more intensive,
both of land and labor,
than we usually see here in the USA.
Every tiny plot, every awkward corner
that produced a patch of hay
had to be harvested;
and everyone, women and children too,
had their vital part to play.

I seem to recall
from childhood hours in Yorkshire
helping on nearby farms
that when hay is ready,
it is ready;
and must be cut and stored
before the rain can come and ruin it.
"Make hay while the sun shines"
is a proverb firmly rooted in experience!

When Jesus sent his seventy
out into the world ahead of him,
he must have known the hay was ready,
must have sensed the wistfulness of heart,
that longing deep in people's eyes
for something true and decent,
challenging, to build their lives around,
something that brought purpose,
even destiny, within the daily grasp

of their toiling, their relationships,
their dreaming hopes and fears.

Those crowds that flocked to hear him—
I'm sure that some came for the spectacle,
the miracles he did, the free food
he was reputed to provide.
And then there were the opportunities
one finds in any gathering for trade or crime,
the gathering and giving out of gossip,
songs and stories, other information.
But it seems that most of them
came there for hope—
walked, all day perhaps,
across the hills to find out
what it was that he was saying,
that he was being, what it was made
neighbors turn their lives around because of him.
They came because they yearned for hope,
a vision of what might be, a promise
of God's aid in getting there.

Those fields were ripe for harvest
and Jesus wished for laborers—
not just to gather in a bigger crop
to fill God's heavenly barns to bursting—
rather because he saw the need,
he recognized the hunger
and the lostness in their eyes;
and he longed with all his heart
to feed them, comfort, strengthen them,
to set them on the way.

As I go forth now to labor
in fields ripe for harvest, Lord my God,
let me share Jesus' compassion,
let me bear something of his promised hope,
let me wear the joy of harvest home at last.
Amen.

The harvest is plentiful, but the laborers are few . . .
—Luke 10:1-2

When I helped on the farms as a boy,
the high point of excitement would come
as a field was reaped,
from the edges in toward the center,
and at last a tiny island would be left
of standing wheat or hay—
an island densely populated with rabbits
and other former occupants of those new-naked acres.
Then, as the scythes approached their final refuge,
the poor creatures would make a break for it,
only to end up that night as rabbit stew
or game pie in the farm kitchen.

I always felt a pang of guilt and pity
for those animals caught in such a desperate plight.
Tonight, in light of Jesus' parable,
I wonder about innocent victims
of the harvest he spoke about.
Not Jesus' victims—
I cannot believe there were any of those—
but folk who suffer nowadays
from the harvesting techniques,
mass-marketing methods, of many
who seek to reap the Master's fields.

I remember from parish calls
elderly widows tithing frugal savings
to support mass media preachers
with already vast and lavish budgets
and questionable lifestyles.
Anguished conversations come to mind,
long-distance talks with desperate parents
whose children have renounced them,
want no contact whatsoever,
because of some dramatic Bible teacher's
application of the sayings of our Lord.
I touch again embittered, faithless lives

which once were pledged to Christ,
yet were so misled by promises,
full technicolor visions of nirvana,
that when castles in the air came crashing down
they never trusted anyone again.

How does one labor honestly
and lovingly within the harvest
to which Jesus calls us?
Surely it is by attending to the One
who sends us in the first place.
Jesus' words and deeds
fulfilled a healing function,
completing circles,
bringing folk together,
opening them up to one another
as children of one heavenly Father.
Jesus' way of life was simplicity lived out,
no symbols of success, excess—a robe
and sandals, staff and loaf and cup—
the lasting symbols that he dealt in.
He pointed people beyond himself
toward the God who sent him;
consistently refused to condemn sinners,
and made of his entire self an invitation
to God's banquet feast of grace.

Forgive me
for the pain, the fear,
the hurt I have inflicted upon others
in these daylight hours now past.
Let me never use your gospel
to promote my own cause.
Fit me to labor in your harvest, Lord,
to wield the mighty working tools
of your mercy and your tender love.
Amen.

DAY ELEVEN
Of Lambs and Wolves
Luke 10:3-16

DAY ELEVEN/Morning

Go your way; behold, I send you out as lambs in the midst of wolves.

—Luke 10:3-16

Not the most encouraging description
for these new-trained disciples
to carry along with them,
to bear in mind as they go forth
to prepare the way for their Master's coming.
Mother Nature, as we fondly like to call her,
generally pays scant attention to
the fluffy, soft appeal of newborn sheep,
or any other infant creature.

Here on the coast of Maine
I have watched a pair of gulls
harassing a family of new-hatched ducks
as they swim along the shallows
of the bay in search of food.
The fearful parents flap their wings
thrusting frantic beaks up high
to drive off the attack,
while all the time trying to prod
their young into a tight protective circle.
But the fiendish tactics of the gulls
set one of them to distracting the adults
with fierce, high swooping dives,
while the other flies in low—
just above the water line
from the opposite direction—
and snatches up a chick.
Inevitably, soon or late,
through weariness or wiliness,
both gulls fly off,
their bellies filled with duckling.

Lambs among savage wolves
should expect no kinder fate,
and Jesus' audience of farmers, shepherds,
fisherfolk would know that very well.

What, then, was the point
of this rather unpromising parable?

Perhaps he wanted to be sure
they harbored no illusions
about the reception they would receive.
For even though they bore with them
the good news of God's kingdom,
many of those who would hear would not be ready,
willing, or able to welcome that good news;
and some, who were invested
in quite another kingdom
would probably resist it
in any and every way they could.

A second purpose
Jesus must have had
for this parable was
to teach his new disciples
something vital about the manner
of the ministry they were undertaking.
Lambs, in those Galilean hills,
must have faced many times
the savage, grim reality
of hunting packs of wolves.
Just like those harried ducks,
the only way that they survived—
at least some of them did—
was by their dependence on each other,
by staying close within the flock,
by trusting themselves implicitly
and completely to the one who
guided them toward green pastures.

Guide me this day, good Shepherd,
to green pastures, clear water springs;
set me safe within the fellowship of your flock,
and deliver me from any who would harm.
Amen.

DAY ELEVEN/Evening

Go your way; behold, I send you out as lambs in the midst of wolves.

—Luke 10:3-16

On the far west coast of Scotland,
most westerly point of the British Isles,
lies a peninsula called Ardnamurchan,
which is the closest thing to *Brigadoon*
that I have ever come upon.

Traveling from the south you enter it by water,
across a narrow mountain-sided strait by ferryboat;
and from that point the craggy bens and glens,
the narrow, grassy, one-way roads
(with occasional "Passing Places")
the dizzying vistas of the sea—
the sparkling broad Atlantic—
and the jagged outlines of the Hebrides
just off the coast, delight the eye,
lay a lilting tune upon the lips,
and tantalize the soul.

Late one midsummer's eve,
the year's very longest day when,
in those northern latitudes,
the sky never grows quite dark,
I stood beside a battered lighthouse
on the most far-western headland
and watched the lingering light
spilling across the outer islands,
turning the sea to silver.

Behind me I heard voices,
shrill whistling and the sound of dogs,
and wondered what children were doing
out at play so deep into the evening.
Then, as I retraced my steps,
I caught an outline at the crest
of one of the nearby hills,
a shepherd with his dog

fetching in the sheep
for an early start on next day's shearing.
They came spilling down the hillside,
single file along their narrow tracks,
the new spring lambs
tucked tight behind their ewes,
and I marveled at the skill of man and dog
to introduce such rapid order to this mass
of independent, rather foolish creatures.

The shepherd with his flock.
As one who bears the name I do,
who grew up in that land which sings
by heart the shepherd's psalm to Crimond
as its beloved national anthem,
what other words and melody
could spring to mind and trembling lip?

> The Lord's my shepherd, I'll not want,
> He makes me down to lie
> In pastures green. He leadeth me
> The quiet waters by . . .

For this vision, Lord,
of peace and tranquil beauty;
for the vision that you gave through
the Shepherd King—the psalmist—David;
and above all in the Good Shepherd—
your only Son—Jesus our Savior;
for knowing you as my shepherd
through all the narrow tracks
and rugged hillsides
of my days;
for all of this I offer
as a lamb within your fold
my humblest thanks.
Now fold me in your presence
through the darkness hours.
Amen.

DAY TWELVE
Satan's Fall
Luke 10:17-20

I saw Satan fall like lightning from heaven.
                    —Luke 10:17-20

An intriguing question Jesus raises
in this parabolic word of encouragement
to his newly returned missionaries.
What was Satan doing in heaven
in the first place?
The popular impression,
so far as I have ever known,
is that his satanic majesty inhabits
a quite different spot,
a place from which it is most difficult to fall,
and just about as difficult to rise again.

In the Old Testament, however—
and that was Jesus' Bible after all—
the Hebrew scriptures present Satan
in more of a changing and developing role,
from that enigmatic serpent in the garden,
to the "public prosecutor" type in *Job*
who holds an office in God's courts
that enables him to question God;
even to challenge the Divinity
about the authenticity of the faith of Job—
the apple of God's eye.

John Milton portrayed Lucifer
as a supremely ambitious archangel,
God's usurping rival, as it were,
for heavenly authority and power.
In narrating his downfall—
Satan's plummeting descent
from heaven's gates
to the abyss of hell—
that classic Puritan poet shaped
our concepts of perdition to this day.

The question is the classic one of evil.
Precisely where lie its origins,

DAY TWELVE/Morning

and just who is to be blamed?
Human nature, with its twists and turns,
its seeming inevitably bent and crooked tendencies,
has always been a leading candidate
in this grim, contorted quest.
Yet there is evil, cruelty, a brutality
and agony within the world of natural phenomena,
for which our mortal nature all unaided
cannot reasonably be held responsible.

Evil, in this century alone,
has loomed so dark across the map
of history that its fell shadow seems to fall
from something, someone vaster, far,
than anything yet seen on human scale.
Even demonic figures like Hitler and Stalin
appear puny when set beside the monstrous evils
that were carried out in their names.

"You believe in powers of good . . ."
said a Russian college professor friend
one day in searching conversation,
"You believe in powers of good in the world;
why, then, can you not accept powers of evil?
Men like Hitler, Mussolini, Stalin,
were not mere demented souls,
deranged and pathological killers.
They began that way, perhaps,
but gradually were possessed by powers
far vaster than themselves.
Perhaps they sold their souls to the devil."

Whatever be the origins of evil
I know its dark attraction in my heart.
Guard me, this new day,
from all the wiles of wickedness, good Lord,
and lead me in the way everlasting.
Amen.

I saw Satan fall like lightning from heaven.
　　　　　　　—Luke 10:17-20

Was this, then,
an intentionally ironic statement?
Did Jesus mean to poke some gentle fun
at the wild enthusiasm of his followers,
bringing them back down to earth
as one treats overexcited children;
setting their newfound success
within the far broader perspective
of the eternal cosmic struggle
between good and evil?

Yet he follows up this saying
with what can only appear to be
a completely serious endowment
of power and authority
over evil spirits.

It seems to me
that Jesus, in fact, shared,
rejoiced in their glad enthusiasm;
responded with an answering excitement
to the news of his disciples' wide success.

That word, *enthusiasm*
means literally, "in-God-ness," after all;
and certainly Jesus was
the most fully "in-God" person,
the most truly *en-theos*-iastic human being
this world has ever seen,
has ever glimpsed God in and through.

The implications here
in this affirmative response
can be surprising and delightful,
suggesting that Satan is dethroned,
not just by piety and prayers,
the daily disciplines of earnest faith,

DAY TWELVE/Evening

but also,
maybe even more so,
by the glad, wholehearted victory cry,
the song of soaring triumph
on the lips
of the conquering children of God.

Might it be
that just so long
as we are willing to put on
the sad, despondent ashes of defeat;
just so long as Christians see themselves
as waging an enormous, agelong battle
against wearying, daunting odds;
just so long as Christ's own legions
are unwilling to look up,
to raise their eyes
above the daily dust and din
and glimpse the banners flying—
those full, bright flags of victory
from the turrets of the King—
just so long
our ways will all be bound
in shadows, doom and gloom?

As I turn myself
toward my rest this night,
let my slumber be in you, Lord God,
and thus be enthusiastic slumber.
Refresh my needy spirit
with the radiance of that vision
caught by John of Revelation,
when the victory banners of the Lamb
will float full and flaunting free
across the parapets of heaven
to welcome home in triumph
the servants of the King.
Amen.

DAY THIRTEEN
About Neighbors
Luke 10:25-37

DAY THIRTEEN/Morning

A man was going down from Jerusalem to Jericho, and he fell among robbers . . .

—Luke 10:25-37

"And who is my neighbor?"
that skillful, legal mind at work,
"desiring to justify himself"
as the scripture says;
trying to show, in other words,
that Jesus' clear, straightforward,
and completely unequivocal answer
to his original inquiry
was not really quite so obvious after all.

That clever lawyer sought
to lure the Master into a debate,
a long, learned discussion, no doubt,
citing cases, precedents, and lawbooks—
chapter, line, and verse—
about precisely what might be agreed upon
by all the interested parties
to constitute a "neighbor."

It does seem only reasonable,
after all; if we are to be commanded
to actually love one of these entities,
we had better know precisely
what a neighbor is and is not;
and also, while we're at it,
make completely clear and fully evident
what might be the precise obligations
that can be expected of one
vis à vis said neighbor.

This is a strategy we all employ;
learning from early years
the ways to postpone,
fend-off by debate,
the taking of an action.
In the United States Senate

74

they even have a name for this maneuver,
calling it "the filibuster."

And it does appear to be
a much safer, more cautious
and controlled way of handling such issues.
For so long as folk are wrangling
over definitions of the finer points
of "neighbordom" they do not have to do
a blessed—or unblessed—thing
about that wounded body
lying there beside the road.

So we join our seminars
and study groups,
we engage in "the paralysis of analysis"
puzzling about just what our faith
might have to say to this or that,
might be calling us to do,
here in this modern age.
And all the while our neighbors
lie untended by the wayside;
our brothers, sisters die
of hunger, degradation, and despair.

Help me to know
the limits of debate, Lord my God,
show me when it is time
to stop and think,
discuss and strategize,
and when to put a speedy end
to such deliberation and to act
in faith and in response
to urgent human need.
In the name of him whose action
took him to the cross on my behalf.
Amen.

*A man was going down from Jerusalem to Jericho, and he fell
among robbers . . .*

—Luke 10:25-37

This classic parable,
for all the centuries of telling
and retelling,
of interpretation and application,
is also ever new,
ever full of fresh surprises.

For one example,
many people never notice
that Jesus does not actually provide
an answer to the crafty lawyer's question.
What he wanted from the Lord
was a precise and narrow definition
of just whom he had to love,
and also, by process of elimination,
whom he was free to hate,
or at least neglect, ignore
as of no real importance.

But Jesus would not tell him who to love.
This parable does not propose—
as many people think—
that love has to extend to everyone,
yes, even to the lowly and despised Samaritan.

On the contrary, in fact,
the Samaritan—the actual neighbor
according to the conclusion of the story—
becomes the helper and not the helped.
He is the lover, not the one
in desperate need of love.

To this lawyer who was set
to argue the untold complexities
and potential legal entanglements
of following the command

to love one's neighbor,
Jesus demonstrated with his tale
just how easy it all can be;
so simple and uncomplicated, in fact,
that even this despised Samaritan,
without any of the glorious benefits
of Jewish law and practice,
could practice it—act neighborly—
without one moment's hesitation
or intricate legal debate.

We are to *be* a neighbor, then,
and that means not to count the cost:
not to sit long in the saddle
worrying whether this lone, abandoned body
might be a trick, a decoy set
to lure unwary travelers to dismount,
render themselves easy prey for ambush
by a band of hidden robbers;
not to calculate that,
should you stop to help,
the probable delay will cost you
precious moments in the temple,
or wherever you are bound.
To be a neighbor is to see
and feel the pain of others
and to risk sharing it for life.

Let me be a neighbor, Lord,
responding to the woundedness of others
as One did who came down beside us,
walked our perilous ways,
knelt in the dust to tend us,
and mending all our wounds
with the gift of his own life
sets us safe within the inn of faith
till we are healed, restored at last.
Amen.

DAY FOURTEEN
Asking and Receiving
Luke 11:9-13

What father among you, if his son asks for a fish, will instead
of a fish give him a serpent; or if he asks for an egg, will give
him a scorpion?

—Luke 11:9-13

"Ask, and it will be given you . . ."
Jesus said to his disciples
in speaking to them about prayer;
then illustrated what he meant by this parable
of parents and their children.

Yet, while the promise is a treasured one,
hallowed over centuries of trusting repetition,
the actual reality is seldom
quite so simple and straightforward;
at least, not in my life,
or other lives I know.

For one thing, it never is a fish
or an egg my children ask of me,
but something considerably more expensive
and difficult to obtain.
And what about those times
when a child, in ignorance
(or not in ignorance at all!),
requests a serpent or a scorpion?
Will she, should she, receive
exactly what she asks for?

In fact, we do not always get our wishes.
And many of the things we do receive,
whether asked for or not,
appear difficult to justify
or explain on any grounds whatever.
Are we to say that cancer,
sudden accidental death,
disaster, blind injustice,
poverty, addiction, child abuse,
are really what is best
according to the Divine wisdom,

and that we will understand someday?

Perhaps I will understand;
but here and now I cannot accept
that innocent human agony has any part
to play in God's eternal plan.
Some suffering we bring upon ourselves.
We inflict much more on others
by our rejection of God's will for us.
But earthquake, flood, and hurricane,
the random and irrational hurt and horror of disease,
these all seem far beyond the reach
of such ready explanations.

What God gives
instead of easy answers,
quick fixes, universal panaceas,
is the gift of love,
which ultimately is the clue to everything.
This is a love that lived among us,
knew in his living flesh
just as we do,
"the slings and arrows of outrageous fortune";
willingly took upon himself
the hurt of all of our rejection
and, while he does not answer every question,
stands here beside us
and goes with us,
down all the bitter ways of hurt and death
right to the cruel end,
and then beyond.

Do not, good Lord,
grant to me every one of my requests.
But let me know your love in Christ,
then lead me where you will.
Amen.

*What father among you, if his son asks for a fish, will instead
of a fish give him a serpent; or if he asks for an egg, will give
him a scorpion?*

—Luke 11:9-13

It often seems to me as if,
no matter how persistently I ask,
I end up with the snake or scorpion.
I can promise God all kinds of things,
offer endless deals, inviting bargains,
yet the outcome does not change one bit.

Even Jesus himself,
for all his passionate pleading,
sweating blood and tears
in one last gasping effort in Gethsemane,
could not avoid the awful fate
that lay in store for him.
Was he, then, proved wrong after all?
Did Jesus live, and die, to curse
in agony these trusting words he spoke
concerning the unfailing generosity of God?

And yet he never said
we would get precisely what we asked for.
Instead he told us God is like
a loving parent who will not respond
with harmful, hurtful, dangerous gifts
to the requests of his own children.
And in this way he encouraged us
to let God know what we desire.

Prayer is not a simple system
of demand and then immediate response;
it is much more of a relationship than that.
a relationship in which,
once the basic bond has been established,
all kinds of things, concerns,
wishes, problems, desires, and dreams,
can be addressed with honesty and trust.

DAY FOURTEEN/Evening

Like all relationships,
this one involves a certain give-and-take.
All too often, however, we become convinced
our role is solely and continually
to take and take and take.
While God exists to give.

My own father gave me
many gifts across the years,
some good, some not so great,
and most I cannot even remember anymore.
One thing he gave that I will not,
could not ever forget. And that?
He gave himself:
his smile and frown;
his dreams and nightmares too;
his open, friendly, optimistic attitude
to life and people; his deep, abiding joy
in his own beloved children.

And this, I am convinced,
is what Jesus meant to tell us.
The gift God gives is self,
God's own true self, delivered
on request to all God's children.
God comes to us.
God joys in us.
God hopes and dreams
and creates through us.
And God would no more do us harm,
for any reason whatsoever,
than a loving parent could ever hurt
a trustful, open child.

Hear my requests this night,
and grant them, Lord, by giving me
the gift that bears all other gifts as well,
yourself, in Christ my Savior.
Amen.

DAY FIFTEEN
Cross Purposes
Luke 11:14-20

Every kingdom divided against itself is laid waste, and house falls upon house.

—Luke 11:14-20

"Can you do good in an evil cause?"
is the question Jesus sets
before his opponents with this saying.
"If I were serving Satan
why would I be healing people,
restoring them to sanity and health,
casting out the very demons
Satan has sent into them?"

Later in his writings,
in the Book of Acts,
Luke tells of a similar response
from a good Pharisee, Gamaliel,
a teacher of the law.
When his colleagues on the council
are breathing bloody murder
against Peter and the apostles,
he argues that they should be left alone,
reasoning that if their deeds
are not inspired by God, then they will fail;
but if, by any chance, they are . . . !
Then they had better wait and see.

At times my ministry brings me into contact
with leaders of other faiths than mine.
My own church, for one example,
has entered into covenant
with our local synagogue,
together with the Roman Catholic parish,
vowing to pray for one another,
study the scriptures together,
grow in understanding of each other,
and work together to dissolve bigotry and fear.

Reading the Bible with my friend, the rabbi,
teaching Bible classes to his congregation,

84

listening as he shares his learned
understanding with my own parishioners,
I have begun to see how ignorant
we Christians are about the Jews,
how little we know,
let alone comprehend their ancient faith
—the faith of Jesus, after all—
and also how much good they do,
help they provide, and love they share.
And I have come to say of them,
as many good Jews said of Jesus in his time,
"Can good fruits come from an evil tree?
Can such fine, loving, learned people
really be cast off from God,
adrift from faith and true religion?"

"By their fruits shall ye know them,"
a lesson taught to all of us by our Lord.
And so with Jews, Moslems, Mormons,
the followers of many faiths,
ancient and modern.
I am learning from the Lord,
to wait a while and see.
Not to assume they are completely in the wrong,
rather to hold tight onto Christ;
yet also to reach out a hand of fellowship,
to seek to learn as well as to teach.
Above all to be ready to be led
by God to richer, fuller,
more abundant truth.

Lord Jesus, make me so secure
in my love for you and trust in God,
that I can enter boldly into dialogue
with all who claim to see God's holy light.
Make me as slow as you were to condemn,
as eager as you always were to love.
Amen.

DAY FIFTEEN/Evening

Every kingdom divided against itself is laid waste, and house
falls upon house.

—Luke 11:14-20

Learning to sail
a seventeen-foot daysailer
off the gusty, rocky shores of Maine
has taught me much about kingdoms
divided against themselves.

Two people in a sailboat
without a great deal of experience;
two somewhat nervous pupils
of the art of going with the wind,
and somehow even (almost)
going against it—
to say nothing of currents,
tidal rips, ledges, shoals,
and sandbars, as well as sundry
other awkward items which are always
in exactly the wrong place—
two novice mariners, in other words,
require, above all else,
to work together.

Cross-purposes can get
even further nowhere, faster
in a seventeen-foot daysailer
than in any other container I have known.
Moving together from one side to the other,
while at the same time handling tiller,
main and jib sheets,
ducking for the boom,
can be an exercise in aerobics
little short of classical ballet:
while the sheer alpha and omega
of getting off and getting on a mooring
demands precision drill and timing
that would put the Grenadier Guards to shame.

All this to say I know
just what our Lord meant when he spoke
about house falling upon house.

The same holds true, of course,
in families and friendships,
marriages too—
perhaps above all in marriages—
and certainly in churches.
We have to learn,
by some miraculous grace,
to move together, work together,
live together, love together,
for ultimately that is what
this love is all about:
more than a feeling, an emotion,
or affection that we sense
somewhere inside about another person;
it is a way of putting, holding lives together,
a choreography of mind and spirit,
a balancing ballet of hopes,
desires, and preferences—
fears and futilities as well—
so that the boat can sail,
the house will stand,
the dance moves on
toward delight and destiny.

Show me, O graceful One,
the gestures, motions, stances,
the steps and handclasps,
postures and positions,
all the intricate coordination
that it takes to share
my life, this world,
in lively love.
Then lead me—graceful—
grateful—to the dance.
Amen.

DAY SIXTEEN
Providence
Luke 12:22-32

Consider the ravens: they neither sow nor reap, they have neither storehouse nor barn, and yet God feeds them. Of how much more value are you than the birds!

—Luke 12:22-32

Waiting early at the dock
in a damp and clinging morning mist,
the calm, flat waters of the bay
barely lapping on the shingle;
sun almost there—occasionally visible
above and through the bank of fog—
yet further out on the liquid level surface
creating secret, shimmering, luminescent patches
hovering between sea and air.
In the receptive ear
the light and lilting melody
of birdsong, now and then accompanied
by the sharp, percussive chimes
of a halyard snapping against a metal mast
from boats moored in the cove.

Then suddenly
the row of punts and dories
tied up against the float
begins to move, lift,
toss, and jostle,
shouldering one another,
boisterous in their places
at the rail
as the swelling wake
of some deep, distant-passing vessel,
rippling strong and steady,
from far across the waters,
has finally reached shore.

Even so, to those alert
to parables as a way of seeing,
clear evidences of God's care,
God's providential grasping, guiding,
molding of this whole creation,

DAY SIXTEEN/Morning

such signs abound, lie waiting
to be seen and heard and held to,
built upon for life;
so Jesus tells us
in these sayings about birds
and flowers of the field.

And when something within
begins to lift and move
and surge toward the light,
just when the mist
seems most impenetrable,
we need to recognize,
reach out and seize the grasp
that greets us there;
and holding firm, bring life
to life,
within the swelling circle
of our days.

Lord, jostle me this morning,
lift and stir,
shake my tethered spirit
on the cresting wave
of your high purpose,
your design.
Then sail me far and wide
before the winds of gladness
and of grateful love.
Amen.

*Consider the lilies, how they grow; they neither toil nor spin;
yet I tell you, even Solomon in all his glory was not arrayed
like one of these.*

—Luke 12:22-32

Mowing the grass—
I hesitate to describe it as a lawn—
here in Maine
is a quite different experience
from the same job at our year-round home
in suburban Philadelphia.

Oh yes, it grows just as quickly,
but the stuff that actually does the growing
is a far cry from that uniform green carpet
I get to trim back home.

When we bought the cottage,
the wild brush and undergrowth—
raspberry, blackberry, myrtle, and bayberry
(plus more than our share, it seemed, of poison ivy)—
came right up to the edge of the back porch;
but by backbreaking clearing
and regular mowing
we have created, over several years,
something that could almost pass for grass—
at least it's green and relatively flat.

The interesting part
is that when it rains a lot,
or I neglect to mow, or both
(which is usually the case in Maine),
given half a chance, the clover (white and purple),
daisies, black-eyed Susans, Indian paintbrush,
goldenrod, Queen Anne's lace,
plus many more whose names
I still have to look up,
are back and blossoming again,
making the yard into the kind of meadow
all those French painters used to love.

DAY SIXTEEN/Evening

And this is not to mention
the baby locust, maple, alder, birch trees,
or the wild rugosa roses with pinkish-purple
or white blossoms and the most handsome,
round, and glowing rosehips.

Out fishing early in the day
I have floated off to windward
of some of the smaller, uninhabited islands
in the bay which are, in early summer,
almost covered with these roses;
and their fragrance,
drifting sweet across the water,
catches one unawares;
fills the senses with a rare,
intoxicating, almost elysian delight.

"Consider the lilies," indeed.
What kind of mind devised a world
which covers itself with bright and vivid color,
perfumes itself with tantalizing scent,
renews its coat of living greens
so readily, constantly, generously?
Surely a mind that can rejoice
in loveliness and liveliness,
in ever changing harmony
and ever new variety,
in the shades of light and dark,
the songs and sounds and silences.

For all the natural marvel
of this earth, I bless you, God,
now at the closing of this day;
and pray that I and all your children
may find our proper place in it,
may quickly learn to care for,
respect, and hold in sacred trust
its wildness and its wonder.
Amen.

DAY SEVENTEEN
Treasure
Luke 12:32-34

DAY SEVENTEEN/Morning

Provide yourselves with purses that do not grow old, with a treasure in the heavens that does not fail, where no thief approaches and no moth destroys.

—Luke 12:32-34

One summer Sunday morning
a year ago, and only a few months
before the Wall came down,
my wife, our youngest daughter, and I
attended church in East Berlin.
The church was the *Marienkirche*,
right at the heart of the *Alexanderplatz*
in the shadow of the Marxist government
and their spectacular soaring television tower.

It was a mellow, elegant old structure,
somewhat battered still by war;
and there were around three hundred
gathered in the congregation.
The soloist, somewhere in the balcony,
sang Bach arias like an angel.
The Lord's Supper was celebrated
in a series of large circles,
standing together in the chancel—
Christi Blut für dich gegeben
murmured across the brimming goblet
by an elder, stooped and worn by years;
like the church itself, a survivor
of the war and all that followed.

My rusty, faltering German
kept me from following more than
one-tenth of the pastor's sermon.
It was on the pearl of great price,
a parable which parallels
the message for this morning.
He spoke simply and passionately
of the urgent need to seize the opportunity,
to claim the pearl,
the jewel of great price,

that heavenly treasure for which
it may be necessary to give up
everything one owns.

I took it for a simple, safe,
noncontroversial treatment
of a basic gospel theme
until, later that same day,
after nine days in Eastern Europe,
we drove our car to Checkpoint Charlie,
crossed over into West Berlin.
And there we read the latest news,
not published in the East,
of thousands of East German families
fleeing to western embassies
in Budapest and Prague,
abandoning all they owned
in their eager quest for freedom.

That simple, innocuous sermon
had been, in fact,
a profoundly skillful meditation
on the very beginnings of the revolution
which, in a few weeks, was to sweep
the entire Soviet bloc.

Grant me, Lord,
something of the vision, the courage,
and the skill of that daring preacher.
Let me glimpse the gleaming prize—
your gift of life abundant and eternal—
then make me brave to act
and speak and live in such a way
that I may claim that treasure
with everything I own,
in everything I am.
Amen.

For where your treasure is, there will your heart be also.
—Luke 12:32-34

There is a kind of Christian
whose treasure is so obviously in heaven
that he or she travels through life
like an alien from a far distant planet.

This saying of our Lord
and other scripture passages
about separation from this world
have led believers, over the centuries,
into a detached and otherworldly Christianity
which is, I am convinced, the exact opposite
of that intended by the Master.
Such persons are so narrowly focused
on the rewards they expect in the hereafter
that they take no interest in,
show little compassion or concern
for the pressing problems and issues
that plague millions here on earth.

Yet there is a valid otherworldliness
that the Lord demanded of us;
a sense of being grounded in
and in constant communication with
other realities than those
that seem to dominate the daily scene.
People also expect this of us.
They look for Christians to be different,
to live genuinely "holy" lives
(whatever that may mean).
Part of their anger at the church
is an understandable expression of frustration—
disillusionment that followers of Christ,
despite his teachings,
seem no better than the rest.

Reading about the monks
in medieval Europe,

one can glimpse, at least,
what people might be seeking.
These men, and women too, lived separated lives
marked by firm commitments, discipline, and dedication.
Where the system worked—and despite abuses,
it seems to have worked much of the time—
it produced a parallel institution to the secular world,
one in which learning was treasured and passed down,
timeless beauty was created and preserved,
quietness and meditation were part of daily living,
and violence was completely abandoned.
The arts of healing and hospitality,
music too, were cultivated there;
the production of good food, fine wines,
hard-wearing, comfortable cloth.
By being otherworldly in this way
these monks brought help and hope
back to the world they left behind.

Not every Christian can,
or ought to become a monk.
We live in a far different world;
yet there is still much to be learned
from those who choose this ancient path.
The daily disciplines of prayer and meditation,
the strong ties of commitment and community,
that dialogue of separation from, yet also
contribution to this world.
We need to take another, longer look
at this gentle way of life that comes to us
from long ago, continues still today.

Help me to practice
that loving separation from
and yet commitment to this world
that was, and is still practiced by the monks;
that was lived out and then died for
on the cross of Christ my Lord.
Amen.

DAY EIGHTEEN
Stewarding
Luke 12:41-48

Who then is the faithful and wise steward, whom his master
will set over his household, to give them their portion of food at
the proper time?

—Luke 12:41-48

I had to call Scotland
at five o'clock this morning,
needed to let my mother-in-law know
my wife's transatlantic flight
had been weather-delayed,
and she should not plan to meet her
at the airport till much later in the afternoon.
She was out, of course,
"Buying some nice fish for her tea,"
as I learned when I finally reached her
half an hour later.

It seemed a little strange
telephoning from an island off the coast of Maine
to an island off the coast of Europe
half an hour before sunrise,
talking about such things as airports,
airline schedules, London to Edinburgh shuttles,
and the fish for my wife's tea
in far-off Stirlingshire.
I felt like I had one foot in another universe,
an alien timetable, a whole different set
of priorities, even principles,
for getting through the day.

This servant in Jesus' story
had something of the same problem.
Each day there would be meals to be arranged,
a host of tasks and duties to be assigned,
wages paid, contracts negotiated
and sealed, disputes arbitrated,
new persons hired, or others fired.
The running of a large and prosperous household
is a demanding, challenging assignment.
And on top of all of this,

DAY EIGHTEEN/Morning

he had always to be ready just in case
his master should return unannounced
to demand an immediate accounting.
He too was living in two different worlds:
the realm of coping with everyday realities,
and the long-term (probably . . . maybe!) setting
of keeping everything in instant preparation
for that promised day of reckoning.

It seems to be all a matter of timing.
If only we knew just when the Lord was coming back,
then we could plan things nicely,
rearrange our schedules for that time.
But this not knowing . . .
days stretching into years, then into centuries,
while still the wicked prosper,
decency and virtue fail, as usual,
to find their merited reward.
And in the meantime,
there are bills to be paid,
a future and a family to be provided for,
a manifestly unjust world to be survived somehow.
Couldn't he give a hint,
provide at least the occasional clue,
to keep us on our toes?

But what if he has already come,
the judgment is in process here and now,
and we can be condemned, or yet redeemed,
in every act and moment of this day?

Master, prepare me for your coming,
renew my sense of stewardship,
my commitment to these tasks you have given me;
that soon or late,
this day or at the closing of all days,
I might know the joy of welcoming
my Lord's returning home.
Amen.

*Blessed is that servant whom his master when he comes will
find so doing.*

—Luke 12:41-48

My hometown in Scotland
dates back to the founding
of the Stuart line of Scottish kings,
when Robert the Bruce gave Bathgate Castle
in the dowry of his daughter Marjorie,
on the occasion of her marriage
to Walter—High Steward of Scotland -
and thus the Stuart (Steward) line began.

Stewards in those days,
and in New Testament times,
were the kind of persons who
not only bore heavy responsibilities,
but also wielded considerable power.

Perhaps if I had that kind of power,
control over all this world's resources
as chief steward of God's household,
then it would be a simpler matter
to see that all received
their portion "at the proper time."

The food is there, after all,
or could be, so the experts tell us,
to ensure that no one ever needs to starve.
But cruelly uneven distribution
seems to be the stumbling block.

Humanity,
while generously shedding
the occasional sincere tear,
has many other fish to fry,
is too caught up with other concerns—
the race for power in all its many forms.
We do not have the time,
the brains, the energy,

the spare cash,
to dry the tears of hungry children,
to fill their empty bellies
with good nutritious bread.

Surely, then, this parable
is directed toward the mighty,
the leaders and the managers
those who set priorities,
balance budgets, allocate the world's resources,
serve as stewards of the nations' treasuries,
rather than at little me.

Yet, where does it all begin?
Where does this dowry come from
that transforms stewards into kings?

I do possess a reasonable share
of time, brains, energy, and even—
if I'm honest with myself—
a little spare cash.
I have a vote,
a bank account,
a mind, a voice,
a pen, a job,
more than enough to eat.
I have been set as steward
over at least one fair portion
of this world's estate.

Teach me, Lord God,
to be a faithful steward;
not just to gain a great reward,
or to be spared the dread of punishment,
but through the overflowing
of your saving, healing, hoping love
and of my gratitude for all
you have entrusted to my care.
Amen.

DAY NINETEEN
Signs
Luke 12:54-56

DAY NINETEEN/Morning

When you see a cloud rising in the west, you say at once, "A
shower is coming"; and so it happens . . .
—Luke 12:54-56

One essential for our time in Maine
we never seem to use much in the winter
is the weather radio—
a pocket-sized device that stays tuned
to the National Weather Service,
with the sole function of bringing
regular updates of the weather prospects
and occasional special alerts
and warnings.

For days that are endured
in office, school, or shop,
the weather tends to be an incidental matter.
It helps to have it nice, but no big deal!
But for days of sailing,
picnicking or swimming,
painting the back deck
or even hanging out the wash,
stationary troughs of low pressure
can make all the difference.

Growing up in Scotland
where summer happens—
if at all—
no more than a couple of weeks a year,
and heat waves
hover in the low seventies,
I quickly learned that weather
was the one eternally reliable topic
for lengthy and involved conversation,
usually in a pessimistic vein.

It is the kind of thing
that feeds the innate, dour Calvinism
of those hardy, but hardly optimistic
North Atlantic people.

In fact, the tale is told
of two worthy elders of the kirk
who encountered one another on a rare,
warm, and gloriously sunny afternoon
in Edinburgh, and their greeting was,
"Aye, we'll suffer for this . . .
we'll suffer for this!"

Jesus points here
to the readiness of people
to see and interpret for themselves
the signs and symptoms in the sky
that foretell the coming weather:
contrasting this with their inability
or unwillingness to read and then obey
the signs of the times in which they live.

There are signs also in our day and age:
signs of hungry, homeless people;
of mindless, insane violence;
of diseases running rampant
and all kinds of addiction;
the neglect of infants
and the elderly;
and all of this existing
alongside enormous wealth,
unprecedented personal luxury,
and a passion for consumption
that has made shopping replace baseball
as the true national pastime.

Open my eyes, good Lord,
to the signs that I will see today.
Show me how to interpret them correctly
and respond with wisdom and compassion;
through him who ever was
and is your sign,
your Word to a waiting world.
Amen.

And when you see the south wind blowing, you say, "There
will be scorching heat"; and it happens.

—Luke 12:54-56

The semiretired owner of the boatyard
here on the island is one for reading signs.
He lies in wait around the workshop door—
among the mushroom anchors, spare oars,
and outboards waiting for repair—
a Down East Ancient Mariner fixing the unwary
with a clear blue eye, luring them inside
to see the walrus skull, dredged up by his son,
Hartley—the current owner—on his lobster traps
some years ago; a skull that must have lain there
since the last retreat of the great ice,
ten thousand years before.

Next he will produce a short length
(if such a contradiction is possible!)
of green plastic hollow tubing; and grasping it
firm between outstretched, upturned hands
he will walk to the back of the shop and demand:
"Is there a kettle o' gold down there?"
The tube does not respond.
The question changes:
"Is there a pot o' gold down there?"
and slowly, but inexorably, the curved tube
bends itself around till it is pointing,
straining down toward the floorboards.

Right beneath those boards
there is a shaft some ten or twelve feet deep,
but flooding water fills it up, fast as he can dig.
"Someday I'll rig a pump," he swears,
"dry the whole thing out and dig until it's mine."

The tale goes on to treasure maps and pirates,
to another trove—a kettle this time—
located off the point of a nearby island.
He plys the tube again, poses his questions,
106

and no matter how close you peer,
never a muscle in those fingers moves
as the green and snake-like plastic
twists and writhes its urgent answer.

Is it all simply a put-on for the tourists—
those ever gullible "summer people"—
or, like water dowsing, is there something
going on here that we cannot understand?
Who can tell? But our storyteller
stands in a long and curious line
of readers of the signs;
those who claim to see, or to decipher secrets
that are hidden from the rest of us.

There are those
who, from the scriptures,
will calculate the day of Christ's return
and then urge their little flocks
to repent and flee for refuge
before it is too late.
Others will forecast wars,
calamities, and natural disasters.
At least some of them are sincere,
but they are playing on that same streak
in the human spirit those elders shared
that sunny day in Scotland;
that trait which welcomes tragedy,
greets suffering as a long-expected guest,
and looks upon its God as the great Avenger
coming in wrath to exterminate all evil.

Lord, protect me from defining you
in terms of my own dreams
or my own nightmares.
Sustain my sleep this night
with the pure vision of your grace
for me, in Christ my Lord.
Amen.

DAY TWENTY
Fruit Bearing
Luke 13:6-9

A man had a fig tree planted in his vineyard; and he came
seeking fruit on it and found none.

—Luke 13:6-9

One of the summer delights
my children have long enjoyed in Maine
is the picking of wild berries.
They grow in such profusion on the island;
glowing there among the leaves
beside the road,
along the path,
behind the beach,
demanding that you stop,
making it impossible to pass by
without a moment—maybe five or ten—
of scanning, searching, finding,
reaching, stretching, picking,
pouring, crushing in the mouth
as singles or whole handsful
up against the palate and the teeth.
There are so many varied sweetnesses:
raspberries,
blackberries,
blueberries,
and even, on a nearby,
uninhabited rocky islet,
wild gooseberries.
(We tell no one else about them,
but boat across there once a year
to fill our pails.)

If there was one sin
that really seemed to anger Jesus,
that he denounced with extra vehemence
in parables and teachings,
it was the sin of fruitlessness.
He described it in many ways,
through various telling images;
but the basic failing
is that of doing nothing;

of allowing the free gift of life,
with all of its inviting opportunities,
its genuine potentials, stirring challenges,
to dry up and wither away.

The causes, of course,
can be many: sheer laziness,
lack of imagination or perception,
or just plain fear—
the sad and paralyzing inability
to face and take the necessary risk
that must accompany all acts
in the world as we know it—
the dreaded risk of failure.

Reading the Gospels,
one gets, at times, the feeling
that the Lord would have preferred
a healthy rogue or bandit,
crook, embezzler, or other desperado—
any kind, in other words,
of positive, active,
seizing-the-bull-by-the-horns sinner—
to the bland and empty apathy,
the listless, drab timidity
of fruitlessness.

Grant me, Lord God,
the courage to take risks
in this new day,
to thrust my roots deep
in the soil of human suffering and injustice,
to lift my branches high toward
the bright and shining sun
of your sustaining light and grace.
And thus to bear you strong
and sweet and nourishing fruit
with all the life that's in me.
Amen.

Lo, these three years I have come seeking fruit on this fig tree, and I find none. Cut it down; why should it use up the ground?

—Luke 13:6-9

Sometimes the things we do *not* do
can prove to be even more costly to us
than those we actually do.

Soon after we started coming to Maine
I was working on my boat in the boatyard
when a middle-aged lady approached
and introduced herself.
As soon as I heard her name
I realized she was a senior member
of one of the most influential fishing families
on the island. It turned out she was also
influential in the island's only church.

She told me they were presently between ministers—
a not infrequent situation among Methodists—
and she wondered if I might help them out
by preaching the next Sunday.
I saw precious vacation hours slipping away;
so told her I would think about it,
consult the family schedule, and be back in touch.

When I told my wife—
who is wiser than me by far—
about the request, she informed me
I had better not even consider saying no.
"Otherwise we can forget staying long
here on this island."

I did the sermon,
turned back the offered honorarium,
and from that day it seems I have been known
not as "Reverend Shepherd" but as just plain "Barrie"
to the year-round island community.
In such a tight-knit, close dependent place

it's important to be careful about
what you do and do not do.

The Christian life has often been portrayed
as entirely a matter of *not* doing,
of basically avoiding sin and evil.
It is as if, at the outset,
we had been issued spotlessly white garments,
and success depended solely upon
our maintaining their flawless condition.

The chief problem with such a negative approach
is that it fosters fruitlessness.
People become so preoccupied with purity
they dare not risk the rough and tumble
of feeding the hungry, housing the homeless,
visiting prisons.
So many of the persons
one might meet in such conditions
are in flagrant violation of God's holy laws,
that we fear any compromising contact.

This fig tree story suggests
it is not what we have *not* done,
but what we *have* done,
that makes the difference.
The unfortunate tree had done no actual harm.
It had never poisoned any one,
but simply stood there,
occupying valuable space
and doing nothing,
producing not one piece of fruit.
And for that nothingness
it was condemned.

Your friendships with the sinners and outcasts
of your society show me, good Lord,
that life is not discovered in
the mere avoidance of sin,

but only in the wholehearted pursuit of love,
wherever love leads, whomever love leads to.
Set me free from selfish fear
for selfless service.
Amen.

DAY TWENTY-ONE
Mustard Seed
Luke 13:18-19

What is the kingdom of God like? And to what shall I compare it? It is like a grain of mustard seed which a man took and sowed in his garden . . .

—Luke 13:18-19

Here on the island
there are lots of mustard seeds, ,
small beginnings which can, and often do,
lead to great consequences.

The other night we watched
The Sound of Music at the Island Hall.
It was not the most professional production.
The pit orchestra was constituted by
a much experienced and forgiving
white-haired lady on the grand piano.
Her husband—the page-turner—
doubled as spotlight operator,
holding in his other hand
a gigantic yellow flashlight.
The stage wings were shaped by sheets
and tablecloths held up with clothespins,
while the dressing rooms were set around
picnic tables near the side door.
Adults and children—
mainly children—formed the cast,
with a ten-year-old girl as the Nazi admiral
and gleeful, mustachioed boys of five or six
the cutest storm troopers I ever saw.
People forgot lines, the singing
was almost invariably just off-key;
yet it was a truly inspiring show.

To watch a community work together
the courage, commitment,
and underlying tolerant sense of humor
of everyone concerned;
the gentle patience of the adults;
shy enthusiasm of the youngsters—
to be in a packed and wildly applauding audience

DAY TWENTY-ONE/Morning

for the third night in a row;
all this was to see mustard seed being sown,
the building of relationships of trust
and genuine affection firm across
the gap between the generations,
the gulf dividing Summer People
from the Year-Round Folk.

This is precisely how communities
are formed and built and strengthened.
This common bond of laughter, tears, sweat,
mistakes corrected or forgiven,
triumphs shared, a common goal and dream
to work toward, was what shaped
and held the early Christian church,
what knit those mustard-seed disciples
into spiritual giants whose names
still cross the lips of people,
light the pages of the history books.

In our pressured, overscheduled lives,
we need to take the time,
learn again the old painstaking skill
it takes to sow the mustard seed;
to do the tiny things, the prayers,
the deeds of love and mercy,
which, taken all together,
will add up to a life,
no less than that.

Lord, make this day, for me,
a day of mustard seeds;
set each word and deed within
the limitless context of eternity
that I might see and act upon
the vast potential tightly curled
and hid in every living moment.
Amen.

*. . . And it grew and became a tree, and the birds of the air
made nests in its branches.*

—Luke 13:18-19

Tiny things can cause
a great deal of trouble, too.
One recent Sunday afternoon,
after a whole week of fog,
we went by boat across to Eagle Island
to tour the home of Admiral Peary,
a traditional family summer picnic trip.

We could see the fog bank lying further out,
guarding the mouth of the bay;
so we took careful compass bearings
on the crossing, just in case.
No sooner had we made the island,
tied up, and walked toward the house,
than the mist came billowing in again,
rolling fast in our direction,
swallowing up boats, buoys,
whole islands in its path.

We raced round the house,
signed the visitors' book as proof
we had actually been there for another year,
and launched out for home
across the widest portion of the bay.
Soon as we left the dock,
the engine started acting up,
almost dying out,
then picking up again.
I checked gas tanks,
the air intake valve.
All seemed in working order.
Yet the motor was struggling for fuel.
Then I noticed air was leaking back
and forth between the gas line and the tank.
A tiny rubber sealing ring had given way
and no pressure could develop in the line.

DAY TWENTY-ONE/Evening

I opened up the throttle,
and somehow it kept running
through the narrow channel
between two other islands,
still holding a slight lead
on the damp blanket that pursued us.
The motor finally gave out about five hundred yards
from the boatyard moorings, and we paddled in
the rest of the way home.

But all that worry, effort, and concern,
the genuine risk of spending a cold night
lost in the fog with no radio or power,
was all because a tiny ring of rubber
grew too old and failed too soon,
before it was replaced.

There are so many tiny things,
all too easy to forget,
that can lead to consequences
way out of all proportion to themselves.
The time-honored, daily disciplines
of private prayer and meditation.
One quiet moment set apart
free from any other pressure or concern
to be with those persons whom we love
and live our whole lives alongside.
The speaking of a single word to counteract
an ugly deed of prejudice or hate.
The sharing of a meal, a book,
a shelter for the night.

Teach me to look out for the little things,
Lord God, and to trust you to look out
that all such will find their meaning
and final consummation
within the cosmic grandeur of your kingdom;
through Christ my Lord.
Amen.

DAY TWENTY-TWO
The Narrow Door
Luke 13:22-30

DAY TWENTY-TWO/Morning

Strive to enter by the narrow door . . .
                              —Luke 13:22-30
Some years ago, while touring the Holy Land,
I went to see the manger shrine
at Bethlehem, Church of the Holy Nativity.
As all must do, I bowed my head
to enter through that low and narrow doorway,
but then emerged into a vast and soaring space
and went to follow other pilgrims
as they made their way toward the grotto—
that humble cave where once Word became flesh.

My mood of solemn expectation
was abruptly shattered by a monk—
of the Orthodox tradition by the look of him—
standing right where all must pass,
and hawking—there is no other word—
loudly and insistently inviting
all in sight to buy his holy candles.
He seemed to fix on me as a likely customer
as I walked hurriedly by,
doing my level best to ignore his existence.
I must have struck a tender nerve
because he bellowed after me
in a rude, insulting voice, calling me,
of all things, "Spiro Agnew."
"Hey, Spiro, Spiro Agnew!"
as if that was the worst name,
the most abusive epithet, one could yell
at what he took for an American.

Needless to say, I felt enormously embarrassed;
such a scene in front of my fellow tourists!
What must they think I had said or done
to merit such a bizarre outburst?
I rushed along red-faced,
stumbling down the well-worn steps
into the sacred place itself.
And there, amid the velvet drapes

120

and hanging, golden lamps,
all the heavy plush and glittering—
for my taste, overdone—ornamentation,
I knelt beside the spot where heaven
touched the earth with untold glory;
and the weirdness and the wonder
near swept my soul away.

Was it the momentary humiliation
that prepared me, knocked me way off balance,
destroyed my normal, everyday assurance,
and sent me staggering in confusion
before the presence of the holy
so that I was laid wide open,
rendered vulnerable enough
to sense the awe and grandeur?
Entering in that narrow door,
not just my head, but my entire spirit
had been brought low, bowed down, abased.
And into that involuntary lowliness
the majesty of God drew near,
came down in healing and in peace.

We all need such narrow doors,
not just to keep us humble,
but to shake us from our shells,
break us loose from the safe anchors,
and cast us—naked and shivering in soul—
before the majesty and the marvel
of the God who comes among us
in a manger filled with hay.

Help me to recognize your presence, Lord,
not only in the "holy" moments,
but also those times when I feel least in control,
when all I have left to cling to
is your redeeming grace for me
in Christ my Lord.
Amen.

DAY TWENTY-TWO/Evening

Strive to enter by the narrow door . . .
—Luke 13:22-30

This "narrow door,"
by which we enter into life,
seems to have a lot in common
with the mustard seed.

The wide door represents
that broad and varied range
of distractions, devices, and desires
we use to avoid the confrontation with,
the contemplation of, reality—
distraction leading to destruction.
So we move from one amusement to the next,
pursue our multi-targeted goals,
check off the daily lists
of tasks and chores we set ourselves,
and in this way can spend
at least three-score-and-ten
(an entire lifetime, in other words)
if we're not careful,
without ever having taken serious thought
about our ending, our beginning,
or where we are right now,
until it is too late.

The narrow door, on the other hand,
leads in through little, ordinary things:
those which, like the mustard seed,
can seem too insignificant to notice,
yet in the fullest meaning of that word,
are in reality totally sign-ificant,
full of signs, everywhere
and always making signs for us
that lead directly to the heart of things.

A dragonfly lands
on the thwart of my canoe
as I paddle—sabbath-morning-wise—

along the shore of a New Hampshire lake.
I can ignore it, frighten it away,
study its odd body structure,
or simply greet it as a fellow being,
fellow-traveler, sharer of this
minute piece of universe;
a sign that points me,
bears me, if I will permit,
into the chain of life,
the turning circle of all being,
that lifts me up and sets me down
where I belong, with loons and larvae,
the sun, sparkling light upon the water,
the young bride and groom whose marriage
I will help seal that very afternoon.
That blue dragonfly can guide me,
through mystery and amazement,
into holiness, where I can lose
and find myself again.

The judgment in the parable
is exclusion—people are "thrust out."
Does it come to that, perhaps,
that as we go through life
ignoring all the signposts,
refusing to acknowledge the quiet
yet persistent invitations to slow down
a moment, stop, and be aware
of what is really going on,
we become immune, desensitized,
shut out from ever realizing
who and where and why we are?

Through this narrow door of prayer
this night, lead me into myself,
my place, my kin, my cosmos,
and my Lord, lead me to you.
Amen.

DAY TWENTY-THREE
The Mother Hen
Luke 13:31-35

*O Jerusalem, Jerusalem . . . How often would I have gathered
your children together as a hen gathers her brood under her
wings, and you would not!*

—Luke 13:31-35

We drove the road from Jericho that morning,
topped the crest of the Mount of Olives,
and parked the tour bus there.
Surrounded by Arab children
peddling their souvenirs and trinkets,
we fought our way to the edge of the overlook
and gazed across to the city over which
Jesus wept and spoke these yearning words.

For all the hype and buildup to this moment;
despite the surfeit of photographs we had known
and seen of this selfsame panorama,
there was no one of my travel group
who was not briefly stunned
by the sweeping vista laid before us,
the rich memory and history it evoked.
Someone—a former choir member I'm sure—
began quietly to hum and then to sing
that well-worn chestnut, "The Holy City."

"What a sentimental move!" I thought,
but then, against my better judgment,
my lingering Ivy-League pseudosophistication,
I was myself, along with all the rest,
caught up in melody and words:

> *Jerusalem, Jerusalem,*
> *lift up your voice and sing,*
> *Hosanna in the highest*
> *Hosanna to the king.*

Yes! There was an exultation there,
an evocation of deep longing and bright hope,
discovered standing at that sacred spot.

I had gone to Israel that January
beset by the frigid inner winter

125

of my mother's sudden and untimely death
just two days before Christmas.
Raw from the emotion-draining visit
home to Scotland for her funeral,
I wanted nothing less than to leave again
within two weeks for a first visit to Israel;
a visit planned the previous summer,
not so much as any kind of pilgrimage,
more a bargain holiday courtesy of El Al
and the Israeli Tourist Board.

Yet as the trip progressed round villages
with Bible names that echoed from my childhood,
among places steeped in centuries of prayer
and pilgrimage, I began to feel within
a subtle, healing process taking place.
My parents had traveled much
in the decade since retirement
but had never made it to the Holy Land.
My mother always said that they would wait
until I, their minister son,
could be free enough to travel with them
and explain what they were seeing.

As I toured the sites where faith was formed
by time and place and history,
as I laughed with newfound friends
and rediscovered old ones,
as I knelt or stood in awe where millions
had done so before, and sensed a gentle presence
close beside me, every footstep of the way,
my tear-washed spirit learned to sing again.

There are times in life when all we need
is to be gathered close and held,
"as a hen gathers her brood under her wings."
I thank you, Lord, for Jerusalem
and for the way you found and gathered me,

and mothered me among those scenes of holiness and grace.
Amen.

DAY TWENTY-THREE/Evening

*How often would I have gathered your children together as a
hen gathers her brood under her wings . . .*
—Luke 13:31-35

Heading off one morning
in our beat-up, mature motor boat
to see the whale we heard reports of
on the news the day before,
we were picking our careful way
between the marker buoys
of a narrow, rocky channel
when we noticed, perched high on top
of a signal pole set on a ledge,
a large, disheveled nest
with what appeared to be a pair
of striking birds standing above it.

As we drew closer we could make out
by their bright distinguished markings
that they were ospreys—sea eagles—
large, handsome, predatory birds
in dazzling black and white,
whose swooping dives from high above
to deep below the surface—
emerging with a wriggling fish
tight in their cruel talons—
have thrilled many a jealous fisherman.
Now these fierce hunting creatures
were surprised in a scene of domesticity.
As one flew off, the other called after
in short sharp urgent cries.
"Maybe she's telling him to pick up
a few extra eggs on the way back,
just in case," one of us joked,
as she settled down upon her brood.

The experience of becoming,
being parents is one which touches,
tames so many of our fellow species.
Ferocious killers can be turned to tenderness

128

and gentle care by the vulnerable presence
of their own tiny offspring.
And the appeal of infant helplessness
can even reach across the species barriers,
leading mothers to nurse all kinds
of alien foster children.

The yearning Jesus talks of in this parable
is one we share with many of God's creatures;
one that can make the heart leap for joy
or ache with dull, unending pain.
To know rejection by one's flesh and blood,
to have to stand by helpless as he risks—
defiant in his newfound strength—
his life, his health, his future.
To watch, with heavy heart,
harsh, constricted throat,
your adolescent daughter walk away from you
in tears, yet still walk away because,
despite the pain, some instinct tells her
she must break these bonds of love
if she would ever freely live
and love in her own right.
Such bittersweet emotions
are the stuff, the daily diet,
bread-and-butter of the parent.

Yet, Father God,
Jesus tells us that you too
share these yearnings,
hurts, and hopes;
that you, just like a mother,
long to gather your own children
in your arms and clasp us to your breast.
Lord, gather me this night
and let me rest within
your strong embrace.
Amen.

DAY TWENTY-FOUR
The Marriage Feast
Luke 14:7-24

When you are invited by any one to a marriage feast . . .
—Luke 14:7-24

So many of the parables of Jesus
find their focus around a banquet table,
a feast or royal wedding.
This mood of celebration and festivity
seems to permeate a whole host
of Jesus' portrayals of the kingdom.

Today's passage contains two such parables.
The first, though Luke describes it as a parable,
seems to be just a piece of practical advice;
but the second is a long-familiar tale
with its urgent warning not to miss
the royal invitation.

Our family was traveling in Europe
during the latest royal wedding
a few summers ago.
The closest we could come
to the actual event was to listen
on American Forces Network Radio
while driving down the autobahn from Munich—
a broadcast interrupted
by the baseball scores from home
and all-too-frequent breaks
for selling soft drinks and detergent.

If we had been invited, however,
unlike those characters in the parable,
we would not have turned it down for anything.
I can see myself in morning suit,
or grey top hat and tails,
royal-crested invitation in gloved hand,
strolling casually in through the great doors
of Westminster Abbey just as if
I did this sort of thing all the time;
taking my seat among the honored guests
away from all the crushing throngs,

DAY TWENTY-FOUR/Morning

the distracting noise of crowds.
And then the parties afterward,
the champagne, caviar and dancing,
bright lights, dazzling colors,
lively laughter, lilting music.

Only one problem looms:
What on earth could we take for a present?
It's hard enough, in these times,
to find something both appealing
and reasonably affordable—
but, of course, not too cheap-looking—
for your common or garden wedding;
but as for a gift appropriate for the marriage
of a royal prince or princess—
I can think of nothing that would be
even remotely suitable.

Maybe that is why
these guests in Jesus' story
one after the other offered up their lame excuses.
Maybe they really couldn't afford to attend
realizing that the only gift,
the only truly acceptable offering,
was a human heart, their own,
broken open by love
and ready for service.

So let me come now
to the great feast of this new day,
my gracious and inviting God,
not looking for a good time,
a splendid or spectacular show,
but willing to offer up the gift
of my own self to you, my host,
and to my fellow guests.
Amen.

A man once gave a great banquet, and invited many . . .
—Luke 14:7-24

Invitations, it seems to me,
tend to grow less inviting with the years.
As a child, one single summons
to a birthday party was sufficient
to maintain a reasonable glow
of anticipation for at least a month;
and during teenage years
invitations served as evidence
of one's own undeniable,
if highly unlikely, acceptability.
But maturity, marriage, and family
can concentrate, and also shorten the list
of options for one's energy and time,
so that invitations come to be evaluated
much more critically and even,
at times, refused.

Looking back over this day,
now drawing to its close,
I recall the many invitations
that I have turned down:
invitations to dinner or to debate,
to dialog, to danger or delight,
to pause and play a while,
to contemplate, to count the cost,
even to the dance.

These were invitations
that appeared to contain
too much of a claim or a demand,
that threatened to take me away from other,
more priority requirements,
my work, my family,
the needs of my own self.

It is not always easy
to say no.

DAY TWENTY-FOUR/Evening

At times the invitations seek to flatter;
they encourage me to feel more important
than I really am, or ever could be.
But I simply have to refuse
if I am to keep my life, my sanity,
those key relationships
which sustain all of my days,
intact and healthy.

Some of these requests
may also have contained a cry for help
or for basic human fellowship,
for a shoulder upon which to lean,
a hand to grasp, a listening,
sympathetic, and judicious ear.
In rejecting such appeals,
am I, at the same time,
refusing invitations to participate in life,
in pain, perhaps, but also in great joy;
in worry and concern, but also
in the happiness of fears relieved,
anxieties dispelled, in all the tangled skein
of threads that weave and counterweave
into the bright tapestry of full
and honest human relationships?

Grant me, O God, to know
how to refuse and how to accept;
the wisdom to know which to choose and when.
Your Son, my Savior, once refused a crown,
accepted instead a cross.
May his example guide me as I move
in trust toward that final invitation
to the wedding feast of the Lamb.
Amen.

DAY TWENTY-FIVE
Counting the Cost
Luke 14:25-33

DAY TWENTY-FIVE/Morning

For which of you, desiring to build a tower, does not first sit down and count the cost, whether he has enough to complete it?

—Luke 14:25-33

The carpenter arrived by boat,
rowing across in the evening after work
from his home on a neighboring island.
I met him on the pier
and took him to our cottage,
explaining along the way
our ideas for the place:
the addition of a single dormer
right along the ocean side of the roof
with as many windows as possible
to make the most of the view.

He looked over the building,
took some preliminary measurements,
asked a few searching questions,
and said he would be back in touch.
A few weeks later the estimate came in.
Unfortunately the roof line was too low
to accommodate a dormer at present height.
It would all have to be raised,
and, with the extra weight,
new timbers would be needed for support.
In short, our wonderful idea
was just too costly for our budget
and we had to give it up,
at least for now.

Counting the cost
was something the Lord himself
must have carried out.
He laid his plans with care
and hard-wrought, earnest prayer,
weighed all eventualities,
assessed the strengths
and weaknesses of the other folk involved,

136

then moved ahead in certainty and trust.
And even though the world believed
that he had lost the day,
that everything he stood for,
worked for, died for, lay in ruin
at the foot of Calvary's cross,
he knew the final triumph, Easter Day.

In another sense, however,
the complete working out
of those carefully considered plans
has still to be accomplished.
That Easter triumph waits its consummation
when the universal kingdom of justice,
grace, and peace will be established.

In that continuing campaign might it be
that I too have my role to play?
When Jesus counted up the cost,
was he including me in his reckoning
of potential strengths and weaknesses?

Bring home to me this day, good Lord,
that even I have an essential part
within the kingdom yet to be;
that each and every human life
has its own necessary role
in bringing in the realm
of God's own peace.
When you counted the cost
and pushed ahead with all your plans
you counted also upon me today.
So help me to live up
not only to the faith I have in you,
but even more so to the faith you had in me
in giving up your life in trust
that I would carry on the task
for which you came and worked and died.
Amen.

For which of you, desiring to build a tower, does not first sit down and count the cost, whether he has enough to complete it?

—Luke 14:25-33

Every morning in the mail I receive
at least one or two amazing free offers,
pieces of glossy paper promising
instant wealth, vast sums of credit,
wonderful prizes, and all these
with absolutely no obligation . . .
that is until I sit me down
and sift with care the acres of fine print.
It has reached the point now
where I simply toss such things away
without even opening the envelope,
much to my wife's chagrin because,
as she regularly reminds me,
if anyone did send a genuine free offer
it would end up in the trash can with the rest.

Although I can't be sure of it,
I suspect things were
not that different in Jesus' time.
This world has never lacked
for crooks and quacks and mountebanks;
those who rob and steal by preying on
the foolishness and gullibility
of the general public.

Jesus, however, never stooped
to tactics such as these.
There were no hidden costs,
no fine print or shoddy salesmanship
where the glad news of his gospel was concerned.
He made the price plain from the very outset;
warned those who heard his message
that if they had any doubts,
second thoughts, or hesitations,
they should not even begin

to follow in his footsteps.

He told them what the cost would be—
a cross, a life, no less than that.
And in return he promised just one thing:
he promised life, abundant life,
his life for them, for us;
his life to live and die
within each one of us;
his life to bring us home,
to bring us back home to the selves
our God intended us, created us to be
before the toil and smear of gain
and greed, deception came along
and corrupted all that is.

We need to count the cost,
just as Christ urged;
the cost to him of what we do
and fail to do each day.
The cost to those around us
of the way we live our lives.
The cost of changing all these ways
and following the costly way
he trod before us to the cross.
And finally the cost of turning all this down;
of saying no to God, and making treaties
with the wealth and eager powers of this world.
We need to take into account the cost
of forfeiting the grace he offers
by seeking cheap salvation of our own.

Guide me, Lord,
to count these many costs with you this night;
to sift through the cheap and shoddy
and find the genuine gold.
Let me be ready now to pay the costly,
yet life-giving price of love.
Amen.

DAY TWENTY-SIX
Salt
Luke 14:34-35

Salt is good; but if salt has lost its taste, how shall its saltness be restored?

—Luke 14:34-35

Last evening I prepared the brine—
salt, sugar, bay leaves, and warm water—
then left the cut-up mackerel pieces
immersed and marinating overnight,
to be ready for the smoker in the morning.
Before seven they had been rinsed,
laid out to dry awhile,
then loaded on the wire racks;
and as I write, the clean, sharp scent
of hickory smoke is gushing forth,
penetrating with delicious flavor
those soon-to-be tasty morsels
of fresh smoked, salted fish.

Salt is a fine preservative.
In the millennia before refrigeration
salt was the only way to store food,
build up a stockpile with which
to face the long and cruel winters.

Jesus, in this parable,
compares his followers to salt,
while Matthew has him calling them
"the salt of the earth."
This would suggest that
at least one major function
of the church of Jesus Christ
is to preserve, hold firm and true,
the treasures, wisdom, values of the past;
all that moral and spiritual nourishment
without which the winters of the human spirit—
the emptiness, fanaticism, and savagery
that sweep across and devastate
our race from time to time—
cannot be survived.

DAY TWENTY-SIX/Morning

I see the church here
on this island playing just that role.
The white, colonial building is simple,
neat, traditional, and homelike;
the furnishings, by no means elaborate or ornate;
the organist and three-or-four-member choir
may tend to struggle, quaver just a bit,
at times, with some of the newfangled hymnodies;
and the preachers as they have come and gone
across the years have not always been
great spellbinders with the Word.

Yet hungry souls are fed,
new faith is found, and fears are conquered;
the lonely, ill, and dying are comforted,
little ones and adolescents find their feet
set firm on the paths of righteousness and peace.
The faithful gather weekly, greet each other,
share their joys and their concerns,
and acknowledge, both as individuals
and as a strongly-knit community,
the divine mystery that calls them into life
and bears them forth again,
that grace-filled wonder
which surrounds even the harshest moments
with a hint of distant, joyful singing.

Make me aware, this day,
of the things that need to be preserved:
this world in all its natural strength and beauty;
the truths and steady principles
which have guided generations in the past;
the stories, legends, and traditions,
images of delight and loveliness
which have led the soul
to wisdom and to laughter;
and the faith in which all these are grounded,
your grace, O God, in Christ our Lord.
Amen.

Salt is good; but if salt has lost its taste, how shall its saltness be restored?

—Luke 14:34-35

This salt that Jesus uses
as a lively image for the church—
his followers in every age—
does more than act as preservative.
I would not be spending hours
with brine and smoke and woodchips
simply to preserve the mackerel
I can catch fresh as sunrise
every morning in the bay.

Salt also adds its seasoning,
lends the tang of zest and spiciness
to everything it touches.
Oh yes, I realize the medical profession
has its questions nowadays about salt;
but it has been prized for all of history
for its power to lend flavor,
to make savory all kinds of dishes,
to bring freshness and variety
to the daily bread of life.

In terms of Jesus' parable,
the salty Christian community
not only has the duty to preserve,
but also to lend flavor, to bring relish,
gusto, zest, to add spice to the dull
ordinary ways we pass our days.
In a grimly practical universe
where utility and efficiency reign supreme,
the church must stand for everything
that may seem to be superfluous:
for beauty, creativity, and mystery;
for the truths that cannot be pinned down,
defined, preserved in an equation;
for anything that still can hold
the power to astonish and amaze;

143

and for gentleness and tenderness,
compassion, all kinds of true affection.

Just last summer, dear friends in France
astonished me by asking me to preach
at their twenty-fifth anniversary mass.
"Such a thing has never happened
in this quiet region of France," they told me,
"but the abbé and the curé do hope you will accept."
So it was I found myself in the pulpit
of the chapel of a small Carmelite convent
preaching the gospel to a community of nuns,
on my right hand; and on the left, our friends
and their invited guests from the town.

The nuns were sworn to silence except for
Mother Superior, who afterwards made friendly,
encouraging comments; and then the "door nun"
who told us how her heart was "sore, so sore"
that we could not share together in the sacrament.
"But when we get up there," she pointed heavenward,
"we'll pray and work so very hard and then
it will so quickly come to pass."

That was a salty moment,
the kind of zesty happening that could fill
Christ's church again with hope and bright amazement;
the kind of seasoning that might still permeate
this weary, jaded world, teach its lips
to frame themselves in song and jubilant laughter.

Renew my saltiness, Lord Christ,
that, after sleep, I may go forth
bearing the taste of heaven on my lips,
a breath of bright eternity to blow
upon the living of my days
and make them glow.
Amen.

DAY TWENTY-SEVEN
Lost and Found
Luke 15:1-10

Or what woman, having ten silver coins, if she loses one coin,
does not light a lamp and sweep the house and seek diligently
until she finds it?

—Luke 15:1-10

Three parables about lostness
in this fifteenth chapter of Saint Luke;
the lost sheep, the lost coin, the lost son.

Interesting how eager theologians
and preachers have been to identify God
with the forgiving father in the third story
and the good shepherd in the first,
but not the diligent housewife
who searches for and finds her one lost coin!
Yet all three incidents
portray to us a God who seeks
and finds that which has been lost
and then rejoices greatly in the finding.

She hadn't really lost much—
the footnote estimates the value
of her silver coin at sixteen cents—
and yet she searches the entire house
from top to bottom, and when she finds it
throws a party for friends and neighbors
that probably cost considerably more
than the tiny coin she had misplaced.

The whole point
of these three stories
is that lost things must be found,
not because of their cash value,
but because they are lost.

Here on our Maine island
that lesson frequently comes home.
I was mowing the turf two days ago
when a wing nut and bolt came loose
from the mower handle and fell into cut grass.

On the mainland one would leap into the car
and go purchase a replacement
for very little money
at a friendly hardware store.
On this island, however,
there is no hardware store—
friendly or unfriendly—
so that any replacement means at least
a three- or four-hour visit to the mainland,
plus return fares on the boat.
One either looks until one finds,
or gives up mowing grass.

Our consumer, throwaway society
makes it easy to abandon
what is lost and buy another.
Yet these three parables
suggest to us that everything has value,
that what seems quite insignificant,
almost worthless in our eyes,
can bring about a great rejoicing,
and that our God,
the housewife of all creation,
values every smallest part
of that creation to such an extent
that she would turn the whole thing upside down
in order to find and save and celebrate.

Help me to see the enduring value
of little things, good Lord:
all those trifles, persons, concerns
that seem to be of no account.
Let me discover in these a source
of true rejoicing with my neighbors.
Amen.

DAY TWENTY-SEVEN/Evening

Rejoice with me, for I have found the coin which I had lost.
—Luke 15:1-10

In all three of these parables,
these stories of losing and finding,
it is important and encouraging
to note that rejoicing shapes
their universal ending.

Losing things
is such a part of being human,
part of the experience of almost every day
as one grows older, more forgetful.
But losing things also lingers
in my memory of childhood days long gone:
a single penny treasured
for all the possible delights
that I might purchase with it after school;
then, standing at the shop door,
it was lost, and I wept great disappointed sobs
until a kindly old man passing by—
probably in his mid-fifties, as I am now—
heard my tale of woe,
pressed another penny tight into my hand,
and was gone—to live forever
in my grateful memory.

The new eyeglasses dropped somewhere
while wandering the "Whinny Knowes"—
heather and gorse clad hills
near to my Granny's house in Scotland—
the threatened punishments,
the hours of desperate searching till,
about to walk dejectedly away,
I tugged a tuft of grass along a railway bank
and there they were, no worse for wear,
and winking in the sunlight.

I have lost so many items in my time
that if ever they could be assembled
148

they would fill their own lost property office.
No sheep, as yet, I must admit,
despite the name,
but pets of various kinds would be there—
wandering the aisles, creating an unholy din;
parents too, and children,
from more than one distraught occasion.
There would be at least one hundred
multicolored umbrellas
and several dozen sets of car keys.
Those times when I have lost myself
would be difficult to account for;
just how would I describe it
to the clerk behind the counter?
And what might that reunion be like?

That is what lingers best of all,
beside the desolation of all losing
there stands the joy of finding, being found.
That dim memory of hunting for one's parents
in a park, department store, or fairground;
the clutching, dizzying panic
and then a distant call,
a familiar voice, a glimpse,
a hand, embrace, and you are lifted
high above the crowd, held close
and told in no uncertain terms
that you are loved, that you are home,
that you are held in joy.

Find me, Lord my God,
this night, wherever I have strayed.
Hold me, lift me, carry me back rejoicing
on the strong shoulders of your love.
Let me share the celebration
of the wanderer's return.
Amen.

DAY TWENTY-EIGHT
Father and Sons
Luke 15:11-32

There was a man who had two sons . . .
—Luke 15:11-32

That's all you need say, really,
"There was a man who had two sons . . ."
and straightaway the old familiar tale
begins to take shape within the mind:
the prosperous, benevolent old dad;
the impetuous, immature, younger boy;
and the dutiful, hardworking,
and obedient older son.

It's all so well-known, so predictable,
so difficult to write or teach,
to preach or even pray anything new,
anything revealing or surprising
about this well-worn tale.
It's all been done before in sermons,
lectures, meditations, poems, study guides—
even movies have been based upon the theme.
What is there new to say about "The Prodigal"?

But what if nothing new needs to be said?
Our society is obsessed by newness—
constantly seeking new and better ways
to do things, make things, sell things.
And much of this, within the realm of things,
may be an excellent obsession.
We desperately require new inventions,
new ways to grow more food,
to house and educate more people,
to fuel our economy without poisoning
ourselves in the process.
The quest for basic knowledge too,
the exploration of our universe, our selves,
is an enterprise we never could,
or should, think of abandoning.
Trouble is, so much inventiveness
is turned to the creation of "new and improved"
detergents, soft drinks, breakfast cereals,

DAY TWENTY-EIGHT/Morning

razor blades, or what is even worse,
to weapons of destruction.

On the other hand, in the realm of ideas—
of concepts, dreams, and aspirations—
sometimes the old can never be improved upon.
If someone finds a "New and Improved" Shakespeare,
Michelangelo, or Bach, I, for one,
will not stand in any line to see or hear.

So, now, it is time to hear again
the old, old story of a father and his sons:
the foolish son—the faithful son,
the humbled son—the jealous son,
and the father (oh that father!)
gazing down the winding track
that leads back to the family farm and then,
at the last, running, racing down the path
with weary legs and pounding heart,
throat so constricted he could scarcely breathe,
to wrap his long-lost boy within his trembling arms
and cover him with laughing tears of gladness.
Next, in tender, comprehending patience,
reasoning with the older brother,
calming his angry fears,
recalling him to the enduring,
supporting bonds of family love
and bringing him also smiling to the feast.

I hope the story ended in that way;
and since God was the father,
somehow I'm sure it will.

Lord, in all I undertake this day
and even if I stray,
watch out for me and bring me home,
to sit down at your reconciling table,
to join with sisters, brothers, at the feast.
Amen.

. . . And there he squandered his property in loose living.
—Luke 15:11-32

Standing on the wharf at Chandler's Cove,
fifteen feet above the water, even at high tide,
you can gaze far down below the surface
and follow the steep, shelving rock face
until eventually it plunges deep
and disappears from sight.
Standing on the point
out in front of our log cabin
you can pick out the subtly varied colors
of rock and weed and sandy bottom
down through the crystal fathoms
and far out into the bay.
And whenever I go fishing
or sail around the islands,
I am surrounded by the birds
and varied creatures of the sea—
gulls, cormorants, ducks, and terns,
the friendly seals and porpoises,
shoals of fish so broad they roll
an endless carpet underneath the boat.
Yet they tell us on the news
our bay is threatened by pollution
and that poisons we cannot see
are endangering its life.

Waiting for the ferry
to the mainland recently,
I watched an aged lobster boat
being loaded—ultra-carefully—
with bag upon bulging plastic bag
until the deck was heaped above the cabin.
"Asbestos from the schoolhouse," I was told,
"all triple bagged. It's been there forty years.
Who knows, might have been best just leave it lie?"

Like that young lad in Jesus' story
who "wasted his substance with riotous living"

153

DAY TWENTY-EIGHT/Evening

(in the gutsy language of the old King James),
we too, in our time, have seized a rich inheritance
stored up over many centuries—
millennia even, in the case
of the natural world about us—
and blown the whole thing,
kit and caboodle, as they used to say,
in one enormous selfish party.

The air, the soil, the water,
even the blessed sunlight we crave,
all the "natural elements"—
as we called them for so long—
are now denaturalized, by our abuse
and long neglect, into a threat to human life
and health, perhaps even human survival.
So it is, that in the closing years
of our century-long feast of "progress"
the tab is laid upon the table,
the long-ignored price for all that progress
has suddenly, and urgently to be paid.

We are learning,
like that wastrel younger son,
what it is like
to have to seek for nourishment
from pig swill in a trough.

This human family of yours, Lord God,
needs urgently to find the lost way home.
Teach us, before it is too late,
to find our proper place and role
as stewards of your manifold estates,
to sit down peaceably together
at the table you have long prepared,
for all your sons and daughters.
Amen.

DAY TWENTY-NINE
Dives and Lazarus
Luke 16:19-31

DAY TWENTY-NINE/Morning

*There was a rich man, who was clothed in purple and fine linen
and who feasted sumptuously every day.*

—Luke 16:19-31

Leaving the supermarket
just a couple of weeks ago,
rushing to make the five o'clock boat,
I was stopped in my tracks by a small crowd—
three or four persons actually—
gathered around a figure
stretched out in the parking lot.
It was an older gentleman
who had missed his step
at the edge of the sidewalk
and fallen full length onto the blacktop.
He was clearly in some pain
and told us that as he hit the ground
he had heard his hip bone breaking.

Someone had already gone to call the ambulance.
Attempts to move him only caused more pain.
A lady brought a blanket from her car,
and I eased it under his head.
More folk were gathering,
including the supermarket manager;
much more time and I would miss the boat.

I felt guilty walking off toward my car,
even guiltier as I drove hastily away.
I realized that there was nothing I could do,
yet felt a bond with those pain-filled eyes,
those eggshell-fragile limbs.
I still ask myself if I should have stayed,
still wonder just what happened,
and pray he made it safely
to the hospital and home again.

I wonder whether Dives felt like that?
Did he come and go each day,
passing by the beggar at his gate,

even calling him by name, or so it seems,
and wishing there was something he could do,
perhaps even resolving to talk to someone,
shift the guilt to other shoulders,
just as soon as he could find the time?

He doesn't appear to have been a cruel person:
he didn't order Lazarus removed from his property,
or refuse him scraps from the table.
Even in his burning torment
he showed concern for his own brothers.
It's just that he *accepted* Lazarus,
ignored his sad condition,
knew about him, saw him every day,
yet did not a blessed thing to comfort him
or ease his daily anguish.
See him now, begging to lick cool water
from Lazarus' fingers, as the dogs
once licked the poor man's sores.

Beggars nowadays, just as in Jesus' time,
have become part of the scene,
at least in our cities.
We see stories about them on the news,
in the press, telling us about their habits,
motivations, daily income, and so forth.
In a society of startling, sumptuous wealth,
we still allow such conditions to exist.
What will the judgment be for us?
Or can we act, not out of fear,
but genuine humanity and concern
to bring these neighbors back
into the family once more?

As I go in and out this day,
open my eyes and my heart, Lord God,
to the plight of my brother,
the pain of my sister.
Amen.

157

DAY TWENTY-NINE/Evening

And at his gate lay a poor man named Lazarus . . .

The rich man didn't have a name.
The name "Dives" arrived much later
in the tradition or folklore of the church.
In fact, in all the parables of Jesus
this wretched beggar, Lazarus,
is the only person who is ever named;
the rest—that lively, unforgettable crew—
the Samaritan and the publican,
those ten virgins, the friend at midnight,
and the judge—have all been nameless.

Why Lazarus?
Why this wretched beggar?
He cannot have been all that unique.
Such unfortunates,
the crushed and broken wreckage of society—
its wars, diseases, accidents, neglect—
were hardly difficult to locate
in that day, or any other.
Might it be that Jesus gave this man a name
because, of all the individuals he described,
this was the most unfortunate,
the one who seemed least useful
or desirable to know?

We make an effort, after all,
to recall and imprint in our memories
the genuinely important names,
ones we hope to call upon at other,
future opportunities:
names of officials or employers,
influential contacts, presidents,
deans, directors, and the like.
But the names of beggars on the street
are not even worth the hearing
in the first place,
let alone remembering.

When would we need to use them?
On those occasions when we pass along
a crumb or two from the overladen table,
it is hardly necessary, surely,
to address the recipients by name.

To be given a name is one of the first
and most enduring things that happens to us.
I can still clearly recall
the Royal Air Force service number
assigned to me over thirty years ago,
am certain I could rattle off its seven digits
while only half-awake, if called to do so.
But a name is somehow more than that,
far more than any label or device
for rapid identification.

We learn from naming our own children
that a name conveys a flavor, takes on identity.
Do we become our names, or do they become us?
A name communicates a person
with all the rights and privileges,
the quirks and characteristics,
possibilities and responsibilities
that are essential parts of personhood.
Therefore when Jesus called this beggar, Lazarus,
he was saying something vital about persons,
names, and beggars, too.

Help me, Father,
to cherish every child of yours as you do,
to treat them with that same unique respect
I so much savor for myself;
to share with everyone I meet
that dignity you conveyed upon us all
in sending Jesus Christ, your Son,
to be our Savior and our Lord.
Amen.

DAY THIRTY
Loaf and Cup
Luke 22:14-23

And he took bread, and when he had given thanks he broke it
and gave it to them, saying, "This is my body."
—Luke 22:14-23

What a curious legacy
to leave us at the end!
No manuscript of teachings,
no list of rights and wrongs,
no systematic ordering and setting down
of all the things one simply must believe
in order to be saved;
but a simple loaf and cup—fresh bread,
rich wine—almost as if he meant
to leave us with a flavor,
a lingering taste along the lips,
a savoring within the brain;
a hunger and a thirst, in other words,
that will not be slaked or satisfied
in any other way than through the reenactment
of this moment and this sacred meal,
the renewal of this presence,
this self-giving passion.

Yes, this action at the supper,
just as much, or even more than any words
he ever spoke, any images he ever set
before an eager crowd;
this act of lifting, breaking,
pouring, giving, sharing, feeding,
nourishing,and making glad,
was one more parable he told and lived,
made real in his flesh;
one last parable to lead us—
eye and ear, heart, mind, and keen imagination—
into the grace and peace of God.

To break bread together,
after all, has been a sacred act
far longer than recorded memory traces,
establishing a bond of holy trust

between the host and guests.
The meals that I have shared—
vast, heaping spreads of meat, potatoes,
gravy, and the rest, hardly to mention
the delectable desserts—
seated at the family table
in the Todds' kitchen, here in Maine,
with Frances's near fatally delicious cooking,
Harold's kindly wit and hard-won wisdom;
these feasts have lent expression
to friendship forged across the years.
They have even come to shape that friendship
into new and ever stronger forms.

Yet even more than friendship
was sealed within this broken loaf.
"This is my body," signified
a givenness that reaches far beyond
the sacred bond of hospitality.
For to all who take and eat
that broken bread in simple trust,
the one who spoke these words
still enters in and opens up
this whole realm of reality
to disclose the richness and the joy,
the design, the daring and the destiny,
the patient, tender, long-enduring,
life-bestowing love that lies
concealed there at the heart.

Break open to me, Lord,
the fragrant, fresh-baked loaf
of this new day.
Reveal to me your living self,
your grace, your purpose for each hour
and feed me with such fragments
as can fill my mouth with joy,
my lips with singing.
Amen.

And he took a cup, and when he had given thanks he said,
"Take this, and divide it among yourselves . . ."
—Luke 22:14-20

One of the never-failing topics
of interest, curiosity, and comparison
on an island, which is seldom even mentioned
in the city or the suburb,
is that of wells and water supply:
whether yours is dug or drilled,
how deep you had to go,
how many gallons you can pump per minute,
their flavor, color, odor, dependability of supply.
The possibilities for fascinating debate
seem almost endless.

Which is not all that surprising, really,
since without that clear and flowing liquid
life cannot continue. We may survive
for several weeks without the staff of life—
the loaf; whereas without the cup
we perish within hours.

When Jesus lifted up the cup
(and it is interesting to note how Luke
sets cup before the loaf, reversing Matthew,
Mark, and the tradition of the church),
he lifted up the liquid symbol of our life
in its precarious dependence.
The following day, his desperate cry,
"I thirst," from high upon the cross
lives out the pouring, giving, sharing
sacrifice portrayed within this gesture.

Yet in giving us the cup
he gave us more than mere survival,
far more than prison fare of bread and water;
the wine within that cup still speaks
of passion and of joy,
the full and free commitment

163

DAY THIRTY/Evening

known in covenant, high ceremony,
marriage, consecration, coronation,
the offering of life in love and service,
the pledging of oneself to another,
to a cause, to a kingdom, to a promise
that is someday to be won.

And there was joy there,
yes, despite the horror soon to be,
despite the presence in that cup,
around that hallowed table,
of pain and bitterness so sharp
that he would ask, that very night,
the cup be taken from him.
For wine brings us to laughter,
making faces to shine, eyes sparkle,
lips to form in joyous song.
So in the cup he pours us
celebration beyond tears,
reconciliation beyond all sad betrayal,
and a vision and a hope so sure
it can brighten every shadowed place
with the radiance of eternal dawn.

So in this final living parable,
Christ leaves us as his last bequest,
life beyond death,
bright joy beyond all grief,
trust beyond reasonable doubt,
and his own self, both host and feast,
presiding at God's universal table
to welcome the whole family of being.

So welcome me this night, Lord Christ;
hold to my lips the cup of your rich love
and true salvation, and hear my pledge
to love and serve you all my days.
Amen.

164

ABOUT THE AUTHOR

The Reverend J. Barrie Shepherd is the Senior Pastor at Swarthmore Presbyterian Church in Swarthmore, Pennsylvania. He has been a guest preacher at Harvard, Yale, Cornell, and Dartmouth Universities and was named James T. Cleland Visiting Preacher for 1987 at Duke University.

Reverend Shepherd holds the Master of Divinity degree from Yale University Divinity School and the Master of Arts degree from the University of Edinburgh, Yale University Graduate School, and Hartford Theological Seminary. In addition to eight previous books, he has had more than 450 poems and articles published. His work has appeared in such publications as *Christian Century*, *The Christian Science Monitor*, *Christianity Today*, and *The New Republic*.

The author is an avid saltwater fisherman and sailer. He enjoys swimming, walking, gardening, and music. He and his wife, Mhairi, have four daughters.

SEEING WITH THE
SOUL

*Seeing with the Soul provides many hours of fruitful prayer and
reflection. Barrie Shepherd unlocks new insights into Luke's wonderful
stories. Perhaps it takes a poet to proclaim a poet's work. When J. Barrie
Shepherd the poet confronts Luke the poet, wonderful things happen for
contemporary Christians.*

William H. Willimon
Dean, Duke University Chapel

In this his ninth book, J. Barrie Shepherd presents thirty days of
thoughtful and thought-provoking meditations for morning and evening
reading. Reflecting on the parables found in the Book of Luke, Shepherd
describes a different way of seeing–looking beyond what the eye can see to
what the soul perceives.

Using as a starting point not only the major parables, but the split-second
images and illustrations Jesus used so many times in his speaking,
Shepherd skillfully spins modern parables from experiences of his
everyday life.

This is not merely a book to read; it is an experience to participate in.
Space is provided each day for the recording of the reader's own thoughts
and meditations about the scripture and about the day's discoveries.

Seeing with the Soul will help readers look at their world with new
eyes–the eyes of the soul.

The Reverend J. Barrie Shepherd is pastor of Swarthmore Presbyterian
Church in Swarthmore, Pennsylvania. His other books include *The
Moveable Feast, A Child Is Born, A Pilgrim's Way, Praying the Psalms,
Prayers from the Mount,* and *Diary of Daily Prayer.* Seeing with the Soul
is his first book to be published by Upper Room Books.

ISBN: 0-8358-0641-3

UPPER
ROOM BOOKS

O9-AOW-565